ANGLICANS IN MISSION

C000227580

ANGLICANS IN MISSION: A TRANSFORMING JOURNEY

Edited by
Eleanor Johnson and John Clark

Report of MISSIO, the Mission Commission of the Anglican
Communion, to the Anglican Consultative Council, meeting in
Edinburgh, Scotland, September 1999

Society for Promoting Christian Knowledge
Holy Trinity Church
Marylebone Road
London
NW1 4DU

Copyright © 2000 The Anglican Consultative Council

All rights reserved. No part of this book may be reproduced
or transmitted in any form or by any means, electronic or
mechanical, including photocopying, recording, or by
any information storage and retrieval system, without
permission in writing from the publisher.

Biblical quotations are taken from the New International Version
© 1973, 1978, 1984 by the International Bible Society, published
by Hodder and Stoughton, except where indicated as from the
Contemporary English Version © American Bible Society
1991, 1992, 1995, used by permission/Anglicisations
© British and Foreign Bible Society 1997.

British Library Cataloguing-in-Publication Data
A catalogue record for this book is available from the British Library

ISBN 0-281-05322-7

Typeset by Wilmaset Ltd, Birkenhead, Wirral
Printed in Great Britain by
The Cromwell Press, Trowbridge, Wiltshire

Contents

Foreword

I am a convert to Christianity from a traditional Chinese family, all the members of which were also converted to Christianity. I always praise and thank God for the power of the gospel of our Lord Jesus Christ and for those who know Jesus personally and took great care in sharing Jesus with my family and me.

My journey from non-believer to believer, on to disciple, ordinand, deacon, priest and bishop continues to imprint upon my heart and mind the prime importance of mission and evangelism in the life of the Church. Thus while I have tried not to lose sight of the 'service and deeds' of the gospel, mission and evangelism have always been a prominent part of my ministry. Paul's passionate cry, 'Woe to me if I do not preach the gospel!' (1 Cor. 9.16), and 'It has always been my ambition to preach the gospel where Christ was not known ...' (Rom. 15.20), have been a constant encouragement for me in my ministry.

The promise of 'My grace is sufficient for you' continues to call me to be faithful to mission and evangelism, while at the same time I know that God, in his own time, will give the increase. Thus I happily and humbly accepted the appointment as Chairman of MISSIO in 1994, seeing it as an opportunity to pay the gospel debt to all those who respond to the call of God to mission and evangelism in the Anglican Communion. I was acutely aware of my own shortcomings in this task, but I was also confident and trusted that God would provide for our needs. Thus the 18 members of MISSIO from different parts of the Communion met for the first time in Singapore (now part of my own home Province of South East Asia). At that very first meeting I praised and thanked God for his abundant grace and provision. Here was a group of people chosen from our own Anglican family – they came with their own credentials and gifts, recognized by their own home church, totally committed to the mission and evangelism process of their own church, eager to be used by God to contribute to the effort of helping the Anglican Communion to turn from maintenance to mission mode.

We met four times in the course of the past five years. We prayed together, broke bread together, studied the Word together. We listened to each other's stories. We debated, argued, drafted and redrafted together. We struggled together to make sense of overwhelming experience and diverse contexts. We offered our gifts and insights to be used by the Holy Spirit. This has been an experience of growth. Our report is but a partial reflection of our journey together.

We are also aware that there are many unsung heroes of faith in our Communion who engage in mission and evangelism in contexts of ongoing suffering and pain, caused by poverty, injustice, disaster, war . . . in short, human sinfulness. We want to acknowledge with deep gratitude and thanksgiving their faithfulness and commitment.

We, the members of MISSIO, present this report of our work. We pray that this record of our journey will be like a Chinese lantern put into the hands of our Communion to light our way to becoming a missional Church. Indeed the journey from maintenance to mission is a long one. I hope and pray our successor, the next Mission Commission, will in due time be another lantern in the hands of the Communion so that we can continue our journey of being a living Church of God in his world.

The Rt Revd Datuk Yong Ping Chung
Bishop of Sabah
Chair, MISSIO.

1

Introduction

Establishment of MISSIO

At the ninth meeting of the Anglican Consultative Council in Cape Town (ACC-9), it was resolved (Resolution 43) to appoint a Mission Commission to succeed the second Mission Issues and Strategy Advisory Group (MISAG II) whose final report was published in February 1992. Among the achievements of MISAG II) was the recommendation of Principles of Partnership (see Appendix C), subsequently adopted by the ACC, which principles were endorsed as guidelines for the missionary enterprise in the Anglican Communion to the present time. The new Mission Commission was to be known as MISSIO emphasizing our participation in the MISSIO DEI (Mission of God).

Mandate

MISAG II recommended, and ACC accepted the following mandate for MISSIO:

- To review mission issues with special reference to the theology of the mission of the Church in a pluralist society; a theological reflection, *Sing A New Song* was published in 1996, and a substantial theological comment is included in this final report.
- To explore and develop strategies of evangelism and development to help the member churches of the Communion in their task of mission; a catalogue of resources available around the Communion and a collection of prayer material is available from the mission and evangelism desk of the Anglican Communion Office.
- To review the ecumenical dimension of mission and to find ways and means for collaboration with other Christian bodies in mission; the Decade of Evangelism provided opportunities in many places for collaboration with other Christian bodies observing a Decade of Evangelism/Evangelization. The mid-point review of the Decade at Kanuga 1995 was a significant event. Extracts from MISSIO's report of that event can be found in Appendix B.
- To continue to review the Partners in Mission process. The process is no

longer used frequently at the provincial level, but the principles have been used in audits at diocesan and parish levels. Note the round table proposal in this report (p. 26) which incorporates much of the process.

- To respond to the requests of member churches of the Communion through the standing committee and to the standing committee's own requests for assistance in identification of needs and opportunities in evangelism and development; networking between MISSIO members has led to exchanges of needs and resources.

- To review the effectiveness of the mission audit as recommended by ACC-6 and to report to ACC-8; this task was overtaken by the commencement of the Decade of Evangelism. The next Commission may need to revisit this proposal.

- To submit progress reports to the standing committee and to report to ACC. MISSIO has complied with this directive from ACC. In addition, there is now a member of the standing committee acting as a liaison person with MISSIO. This person will personally present regular reports. MISSIO has also forwarded proposals to ACC-11 for an Anglican congress in 2003 and a synodical and voluntary mission agencies conference in 2001.

Meetings

MISSIO has met four times: on 3–11 November 1994 at Singapore; on 16–26 January 1996 at Ely in the UK; on 5–12 September 1997 at Recife in Brazil; and finally on 12–24 April 1999 at Harare in Zimbabwe.

Membership

The following is a list of members of the Commission and their positions within their churches. Where no dates are indicated the members attended all four meetings of the Commission. Members who attended later meetings were replacements for members unable to attend, often because of pressures within their local situations.

The Revd Canon Dr Sebastian Bakare	Ecumenical Senior Chaplain: University of Zimbabwe, Province of Central Africa (1997/99)
The Revd Roger Chung	Provincial Evangelism Co-ordinator and parish priest,

	Mauritius: Province of the Indian Ocean, and ACC representative
Mr John Clark	Secretary, Partnership for World Mission: Church of England
The Revd Canon Harold Daniel	Provincial Mission Co-ordinator and parish priest: Church in the Province of the West Indies
The Rt Revd Jason Dharmaraj	Bishop of Tirunelveli: Church of South India (1994/96)
The Rt Revd Riah Abu El-Assal	Bishop of Jerusalem: Episcopal Church in Jerusalem and the Middle East (1994/96)
Dr Eleanor Johnson	Director for Mission: Anglican Church of Canada
The Rt Revd Benjamin Kwashi	Bishop of Jos: Church of Nigeria (1996)
The Revd Paul Kwong	Ming Hua Theological College: Hong Kong Sheng Kung Hui (1994/96)
The Rt Revd Brian Kyme	General Secretary, Anglican Board of Mission, Australia: Anglican Church of Australia
Mrs Margaret Larom	Global Mission Department: ECUSA
The Revd Lionel Longarata	General Secretary, Melanesian Board of Mission: Church of the Province of Melanesia (1999)
The Revd Canon Patrick Mauney	Global Mission Department: ECUSA (1994/96/99)
The Revd Mike McCoy	Theological Education Co-ordinator, Diocese of Bloemfontein: Church of the Province of Southern Africa (1994)
The Revd Stephen Mung'oma	Provincial Co-ordinator of

	Mission and Evagelism: Church of the Province of Uganda (1994/96)
The Rt Revd Jubal Neves	Bishop of South Western Brazil: Igreja Episcopal Anglicana do Brasil
The Revd Charles Odurkami	Provincial Co-ordinator of Mission and Evangelism: Church of the Province of Uganda (1999)
The Revd Dr Michael Poon	Parish priest and missiologist: Hong Kong Sheng Kung Hui (1997)
The Revd Sam Sahu	Provincial Mission and Evangelism Co-ordinator: Church of the Province of Melanesia (1994)
The Revd Canon Ron Taylor	General Secretary, New Zealand Board of Mission: The Anglican Church in Aotearoa, New Zealand and Polynesia
The Revd Dr Hugo Vergara	Provincial Co-ordinator of Mission and Evangelism and parish priest: Argentina Iglesia Anglicana del Cone Sur de America (1994/96)
The Rt Revd Yong Ping Chung	Bishop of Sabah: Church of the Province of South East Asia

Consultants

The Revd Canon Peter Price	General Secretary, United Society for the Propagation of the Gospel: Church of England (1994) (observer 1996)
The Revd Mike McCoy	Theological Education Co-ordiator, Diocese of Bloemfontein: Church of the Province of Southern Africa (1996/99)
The Revd Dr Sebastiao Gameleira	Professor, Theological Seminary of Brazil (1997)

Staff

The Revd Canon Dr Cyril Okorocha	Director for Mission and Evangelism: Anglican Communion Office (1994/96/97)
The Revd Canon John Peterson	Secretary General, Anglican Communion Office (1999)
Miss Marjorie Murphy	PA, Mission and Evangelism Affairs: Anglican Communion Office
Miss Lily Pereboom	Volunteer (1996)

The Revd Canon Dr Cyril C. Okorocha, Director for Mission and Evangelism, assisted by Miss Marjorie Murphy, served MISSIO as its secretary until late 1997. To echo the report of Section II of the Lambeth Conference 1998, Dr Okorocha gave outstanding leadership during the Decade of Evangelism. He was elected Bishop of Owerri and installed in that office in 1998. Since his departure from the ACO, Canon John Peterson has acted in the role of director, and Miss Marjorie Murphy has efficiently attended to the administration needs, of MISSIO. The appointment of a new senior-level mission staff person is expected to follow the meeting of ACC-11 in September 1999.

The members of MISSIO wish to record their particular gratitude for Dr Okorocha's creative leadership and for his entrepreneurial gifts as evidenced by his convening of G-CODE 2000 at Kanuga. We appreciate his theological expertise and his literary skills as seen in *The Cutting Edge of Mission*, in *Vision Bearers* and other publications. As Archbishop Robin Eames has said, 'Dr Okorocha's contribution to the life of our Communion has been immense.'

Lambeth 1988 called for the 1990s to be a Decade of Evangelism. It has proved a turning point for the Communion. The present report builds on the report of the mid-point review at Kanuga, USA in September 1995 entitled *The Cutting Edge of Mission*. This final report not only reports on the movement from maintenace to mission throughout the Communion, but goes further in taking up the Lambeth call for transformation. MISSIO calls the Church to be a missional Church, the life and witness of which will be a proclamation of the good news.

Reports

MISSIO has reported to the joint standing committee of the ACC and the primates, and to the Lambeth Conference 1998. This final report is submitted to ACC-11.

MISSIO, at its final meeting, continued to envisage a future Anglican congress, now contemplated for the year 2003. Before then, MISSIO hopes for a conference of synodical and voluntary mission agencies in 2001. The valuable interaction between the members of MISSIO around the world needs to be experienced by a wider cross-section of the Communion.

MISSIO forwarded a proposal to ACC-10 (Panama) for a 'Year of Jubilee in 2000' in support of international and ecumenical movements for the remission of the debts of the world's poorest nations. This report urges the Communion to follow the lead of the bishops at Lambeth 1998 in supporting the Jubilee.

The fourth meeting of MISSIO in April 1999 took place in Africa – a meeting point of the traumas besetting planet Earth. The HIV/AIDS pandemic, civil war, genocide, poverty, drought and famine are all experienced in one part or another of the largest continent. But Africa is also the centre of revival and home to churches in growth mode, in contrast to many in the 'North'. Much of the Communion comes from Africa. MISSIO was deeply humbled by the evidence of church growth and by the deep commitment of African Christians.

This final report of MISSIO calls the Anglican Communion to continue to participate in the MISSIO DEI and to allow itself to be transformed by the presence of Jesus Christ in the power of the Holy Spirit, that we may become an effective instrument for the transformation of God's world. With this prayer, we offer the report of our work and fellowship to our fellow Anglicans.

2

Engaging with the
Local Mission Context

Members of MISSIO were appointed for a period of five years during which four meetings were held. It was agreed at the first meeting that thinking about mission, and developing strategies or programmes to assist the Anglican Communion in promoting its mission and evangelistic work, would be facilitated and enriched by exposure to the varied contexts in which the Church was engaged in mission.

Therefore, MISSIO decided against solely a conference room approach to its work, opting instead to spend some time at each of its meetings observing the mission work of the local church. The enabled local churches to offer their insights, while MISSIO learned significant lessons through this engagement in different contexts. At the same time, MISSIO members were able to give support and encouragement to their brothers and sisters on the local scene. This sense of partnership developed over the five-year period and the diversity of the contexts contributed to the enlarging of MISSIO's vision.

A brief account of this process of engaging the local context will be helpful to the understanding of this report.

Singapore, September 1994

In Singapore, MISSIO members worshipped and ministered in local congregations on the Sunday of their stay. The vibrancy of the worship services and the priority given to mission and evangelism by these growing churches were a source of inspiration. Given the multi-ethnic, multi-religious nature of that part of the world, special attention was given to unreached peoples, and this was highlighted in a presentation to MISSIO by a local clergyperson. The church was involved in mission to the neighbouring countries, with church members joining short-term mission teams. The diocese places a strong emphasis on the theological and practical training of the laity for such mission work. MISSIO was hosted for dinner by the diocese and the bishop and other lay persons had the opportunity to extend a welcome and to speak of their work.

Ely, England, January 1996

The Ely meeting, held in the winter, did not provide the opportunity for the extensive interaction with local congregations, as was the case in Singapore. However, members shared in the worship at the cathedral, and also attended evensong at King's College, Cambridge. Guided tours of Ely Cathedral and Westminster Abbey gave the group a rich sense of the history of the Anglican Church in England. Visits to Church House (office of the Church of England General Synod), Lambeth Palace (residence of the Archbishop of Canterbury) and Partnership House (Anglican Communion Office) and (centre of Church of England international mission agencies) in London showed the agencies and structures supporting the Church's mission.

Recife, Brazil, September 1997

Because there have been very few Anglican Communion meetings in Brazil, it was decided to hold the third meeting in Recife. The difficulties of meeting in Brazil in terms of cost were overcome in part by the generosity of the Brazilian Church in providing hospitality. The group was welcomed with open arms by the local church, and members were privileged to worship and minister in several churches. The Bishop of Recife, the Provincial Secretary and other members of the clergy and laity were always on hand to assist MISSIO in carrying out its work. From the first day, when a visit was made to a small mission in order to see the work among people who live and earn their livelihood on a garbage dump, the group knew that the Brazil experience would contribute significantly to the spirit and content of its interim report.

The presence of a local priest-theologian as missiological consultant to MISSIO was a great asset to the deliberations in the Brazilian context. Further visits to churches and church events in the evenings after an intense day's work allowed MISSIO members to hear the stories and feel the heartbeat of the Anglican

Church in this part of Brazil. The growing churches of Brazil reinforced a truth often expressed, that churches engaged in mission and evangelism must always be open to change – change in structure, change in style of worship and change in programmes. When new members of varying backgrounds are constantly being added to the Church, the traditional way of doing things will constantly be challenged. Resistance to change in such a situation will retard the growth and vitality of the Church.

Dispersed accommodation, coupled with the hosting of evening meals in a variety of locations, made for long days with perhaps not enough rest. News that the contract of the Director of Mission and Evangelism at the Anglican Communion Office was not being renewed, and fears of the termination of MISSIO's assignment, hindered the group's productivity. However, the visible connection between evangelism and social action, geared at transforming the unjust structures that perpetuate poverty in the Brazilian situation, was inspiring.

Harare, Zimbabwe, April 1999

Following the pattern of previous meetings, exposure to the context was regarded as an essential feature of the meeting. The Organizational Training and Development Centre, which was chosen as the venue for the meeting, provided ideal conditions for a high level of productivity. The pleasant surroundings, the good weather conditions, the suitability of the conference room facilities and the co-operation and friendliness of the staff of the Centre, were all conducive to work.

MISSIO was pleased to have the Secretary General of the Anglican Communion present for most of its meeting, as well as Ms Maureen Sithole, liaison member from the ACC standing committee. Special note must be made of the presence at the meeting in its early stages of Archbishop Khotso Makhulu, who readily entered into the discussions and made contributions that were much appreciated. Bishop Jonathan Siyachitema of the diocese of Harare also visited and spoke of the work of his diocese. A member of MISSIO, Sebastian Bakare, now Bishop of Manicaland, provided further insights about the church in Zimbabwe and the country in general.

Weekend visits were made by MISSIO members to three of the four dioceses in Zimbabwe. Some members remained in Harare, while some travelled by road to Manicaland, and others by air to Bulawayo in the diocese of Matabeleland.

The stories brought back from these visits are too numerous to be told, but they speak eloquently of the many faces of Zimbabwe. There were churches with all the signs of colonial wealth and grandeur, and others in desperate need of very basic facilities. There were the traditional English Anglican services, 1662 Prayer Book and Hymns Ancient & Modern, and there were services in local languages with the revised liturgy of the province, where the use of drums and marimbas brought an African flavour to the worship. In every case, however, the Anglican ethos was evident.

One cannot think of mission in the Zimbabwean context without confronting the divisive issues of colour, race, tribe, class, wealth and poverty. One cannot avoid facing the devastating effects of the HIV/AIDS pandemic. The figures vary, but the death toll ranges between 1,000 and 1,500 per week, with some 2,000 new cases every week. Funerals occupy a great deal of the time of the clergy, and according to one priest, there is hardly a home he visits that does not have someone infected with AIDS. Doing mission in this context requires a theology that is relevant to these issues.

MISSIO was impressed by the vitality of the churches and the courage of the clergy and lay people in facing the many challenges. There was a case reported of a priest who had 64 congregations in the parish, but who carefully organized his work by dividing the parish into zones. The Mothers' Union was reported to be 10,000 strong in the Harare diocese, raising again the issue of the place of women in ministry. There are no women priests as yet in this province.

Recommendation

MISSIO is satisfied that its decision to meet each time in a different location, and to take time to engage with the local Anglican community, has increased its understanding of the mission challenges and tasks around the Communion. The context in which one does mission contributes in no small measure to the theology of mission and the agenda for mission. MISSIO therefore recommends this way of working to those who will serve on the Commission in the future, and draws to the attention of other committees, commissions and networks of the Communion, this model of working.

3

Transformed and Sent: Reflections on Dimensions of Anglican Mission

How can they hear without someone preaching to them? (Romans 10.14)

Do not conform any longer to the pattern of this world, but be transformed by the renewing of your mind. Then you will be able to test and approve what God's will is – his good, pleasing and perfect will. (Romans 12.2)

Anglicans in Mission: The 1998 Lambeth Conference and Beyond

The 1998 Lambeth Conference, through its Section reports, has given our Communion rich resources for reflection and faithful action. They deserve close study as we continue our long and sometimes difficult journey towards being a transformed and transforming Church – that is, to being a people serving the mission of God in Christ.

MISSIO has received with special appreciation the report of Section II, *Called to Live and Proclaim the Good News*. MISSIO gladly endorses the bishops' insights and recommendations, and commends them to every part of the Anglican Communion for study and appropriate implementation.

Rather than cover the same ground, this section of MISSIO's report focuses on matters which the Lambeth Conference did not address, or which MISSIO believes deserve further reflection. We have also posed questions throughout this section which we hope will stimulate reflection and action.

Mission: On Paper or on the Ground?

Meeting in Harare, Zimbabwe, MISSIO experienced its fourth and final meeting as the coming together of joy and pain. The joy came from a sense that its members have learnt to work together creatively and productively, and to celebrate the unity-in-diversity that comes from being Anglicans who are committed to mission from everywhere to everywhere. It also came from hearing one another's stories from around the Communion of local churches seeking to live and proclaim the gospel faithfully.

The pain came from hearing other stories, those of struggle and suffering, as people have had to face great hardship, opposition or discouragement. Several MISSIO members were absent from our final meeting because situations of conflict, violence or illness compelled them to stay at home. In Zimbabwe we saw poverty and inequality, much of it the legacy of the past, but much of it perpetuated by the burden of international debt and by political and economic mismanagement. And we were reminded of people and communities all over the world suffering the effects of war, persecution, oppression, famine and the HIV/AIDS pandemic.

As we prayed together each day in our conference centre on the northern outskirts of Harare, we remembered people in Kosovo, southern Sudan, central Tanzania, Indonesia and elsewhere. Many of them faced death or dislocation even as we sat around our tables, discussing the order of words on paper.

So we offer these reflections, and this whole report, conscious that we are servants of all God's people around the Anglican Communion, and that what we say on paper needs to speak to those who are actually walking the holy ground of God's mission, wherever they may be, and whatever the particular opportunities or dangers they face.

> In your context, does 'mission on the ground' mean dealing with suffering, conflict, oppression, poverty or any other circumstances which bring death rather than life? If so, how can you share your burden with others in the family of God? If not, how can you stand in solidarity with those who carry that kind of cross?

Mission as Transformation

Taking its cue from the presidential address of the Archbishop of Canterbury, the 1998 Lambeth Conference expressed strong support for the suggestion that the transformation of the Church was a priority. However, there was little support for the idea, suggested by MISSIO at its third meeting, that the Decade of Evangelism be followed by a Decade of Transformation – perhaps because there was a reluctance to have a decade of anything.

Decade or not, the process of transformation, begun by the fact that we are in Christ, needs to continue to reshape our communities and institutions, so that our Communion itself is a proclamation of the gospel. 'We must walk the walk to talk the talk.'

The report of Section II of the 1998 Lambeth Conference begins with an affirmation that mission is God's way of loving and serving the world. The sending God sent the people of God to participate in the mission of God. Section II also emphasizes that the aim of God's mission is the transformation of the life not only of individuals but also of society, nations and the created order (cf. John 10.10).

The Church (*ekklesia*) is the community called out of the world to be the instrument of God's mission. If the medium is to be the message (Marshall McLuhan), only a Church which is itself always in the process of being transformed can fulfil such a calling. As MISSIO spelt out at its second meeting (Ely 1996), '[The Church] must give increasing attention to the relation between mission and culture; have a more integrated understanding of the relation between justice and the gospel; and show awareness of the reality of structural sin as well as personal sin.'

What, in your own church, needs to be transformed? How might that transformation take place?

Transforming or conforming?

The transforming gospel addresses both personal and structural sin.[1] We cannot reduce evangelism to the transmission of a set of articles of faith without any sense of urgency to incarnate that faith in a world beset by injustice and oppression. Salvation, the biblical idea of wholeness or health, is too often reduced to the saving of souls rather than the whole person; and sin is seen as exclusively moralistic and individualistic, needing absolution from personal guilt. The call of conversion is often addressed exclusively to individuals without any reference to the corporate dimension – yet many people are both sinners and the sinned-against.

The vision of the missionary Church is to work with God to re-invent the structures of human society so that they more closely reflect the purposes of God.[2] The awareness of the socio-political dimension of evangelization[3] needs to be brought into the every-day life of congregations if we are to live as agents of transforma-tion. 'The Gospel is about salvation from sin. But it is more than my personal salvation ... The salvation which Jesus promised was the coming of God's kingdom.'[4]

Transforming mission does not just lead people to experience Christ, but to experience him in such a way that their faith com-munities experience both renewal and transformation. Many committed Christian students, for example, drift into nominalism within a few years of leaving university. The challenge here is to see mission as formative and transformative rather than just con-verting.[5]

Christianity is not simply a religion. The first Christians were called 'followers of the way'. They were a transforming force in apostolic times. Their concern was not only to 'talk the talk', but to 'walk the walk'. Transformation in this light means action to establish conditions where wholeness of life may be enjoyed.[6] While the word 'development' might suggest that communities can reach a satisfactory level of growth, 'transformation' suggests that growth does not end – that it continues until 'the kingdom of the world has become the kingdom of our Lord and of his Christ' (Rev. 11.15).

To 'walk the walk' means that disciples of Jesus follow the way of the cross. 'The church on earth, as the church *in via* (on the way) remains marked by the sins of humankind and by its solidarity with the sufferings of the world ... Sharp things that divide us can paradoxically turn out to be gift ... The world is not used to such a possibility as this: that those on opposing sides should stay together ... bearing each other's burdens, even entering one another's pain.'[7]

This takes us to the heart of *koinonia* that is participation in the life of the crucified one (cf. Phil. 2.6–8). The extent to which the Church is seen to be one with human suffering is a telling sign of its identity as the body of Christ.[8] A transformed Church will, like the individual disciple, bear the marks of the Lord Jesus (cf. Gal. 6.17).

If you were to begin the journey to becoming a transformed Church, how would you manage the pain of change, the conflict caused, the insecurity which many would feel?

The Church and the kingdom/reign of God

Jesus came to announce the reign of God (Mark 1.14–15). This is the 'good news'. In Jesus' ministry, death and resurrection, the coming reign of God becomes a present reality.

The Church demonstrates this reality, as it:

- offers life, not death
- includes rather than excludes
- aims for wholeness and health
- lives by values that are different from those of 'the world'
- emphasizes service rather than domination.

The agenda of the Church is rooted in the Old Testament (e.g. Lev. 25, Isa. 65.17–25) and finds expression in the New Testament (e.g. Acts 2.42–7). The notion of the Jubilee or 'year of favour' is fundamental to the good news (Luke 4.18–19; cf. Isa. 61.2). It is a time for remission of debt, freeing economic captives, enabling refugees to return home, and returning land and resources to the displaced. These marks of mission are made known in the advent of Jesus. The good news is Emmanuel, the God-of-love-and-justice-with-us. The promotion of the Year of Jubilee in 2000 is a significant and ecumenical mission event. We welcome the support given to it by the 1998 Lambeth Conference; we are grateful to hear of those provinces and mission agencies/boards which have already committed themselves to it; and we challenge other provinces and mission agencies/boards to make it one of their priorities.

The Church cannot proclaim this good news simply by 'having a mission' or by seeing mission as an external activity or programme. To put it more positively: the Church must be mission – a community that incarnates the mission entrusted to Jesus and given by him to his followers (John 20.21). The world will never hear a gospel that is apparently contradicted by the character of the community that proclaims it. A profoundly transformed Church alone can be God's agent of transformation.

Review the mission activities and priorities of your province (or diocese or parish). How do they relate to the rest of the

Church's activities and priorities? To what extent do they arise out of your identity as the people of God, or out of the pressures of your context? How integrated are they with your liturgical life and patterns of ministry?

The identity and character of the Church in mission

'Only by constantly recalling that its true identity is Christ alone can the church escape from being just another religious institution. In her form ... that is exactly what she is – a creed, a cult and a code of behaviour, with pundits, priests and prelates to manage them ... Only by being Christ himself can the Christian community remain the source of that living water which is also the wine of life.'[9]

When we use the Pauline image of 'the body of Christ' we may be referring to the incarnate Christ, to the eucharistic body or to the mystical body, the Church. The three are, of course, intimately connected. The Church is the sacrament of the gospel. The Church is the mission of God because it is the expression and instrument of the Sent One.

There can be no renewed mission if eyes do not meet in friendship, welcome, understanding and kindness.[10] The early Church knew that *chrestos* ('kindness') was only a vowel away from *Christos*. Respect, courtesy, kindness and gentleness must be features of the structures through which the grace of God is communicated.

How is the Church in your context living as a sacrament of the gospel?

The emerging Church

There are signs that the transformation of churches is under way as we approach the third millennium. This is a particularly acute issue for churches in the First World, where many are trying to disentangle themselves from top-heavy and inflexible structures, from resources locked into expensive maintenance of plant, and from 'background' values shaped by the assumptions of modernism. Among others, the Alban Institute in the USA has been a pioneer in this movement, while the ecumenical Center for Parish Development in Chicago focuses on helping parishes to plan for transformational change. In Britain, theologians such as Robert

Warren[11] and Robin Greenwood[12] are also creatively addressing the issues of transformation.

Around the Anglican Communion, the movement known as 'Total Ministry' – that is, teams of lay and ordained people sharing responsibilities formerly undertaken by lone clergy, is gaining momentum. Some mission agencies (such as the Anglican Board of Mission, Australia) are seeking to model this approach through team structures.

Where do you see signs of a Church emerging that is more participatory and less hierarchical, more communal and less institutional? What signs do you see that the Church in your area is better able to proclaim the reign of God in its life and witness?

The Church in Mission: Doing, Having, Being

The challenge to be faithful witnesses to God's transforming mission means that we have to rethink how we live out that mission.

It has been suggested that, whereas the Church of the Christendom period did mission, and the Church of the Enlightenment and modern periods had a mission, the emerging Church is mission. This may be largely true of the 'old' churches of Europe and North America. Churches which have always lived as minorities, especially in the Two-Thirds World, have long known that they are 'mission churches' in this sense. But churches which have traditionally seen themselves as sending churches are also called to the new identity which they share with local churches everywhere: to be sent churches.[13]

Who we are is integral to how we witness to the good news. God invites us – as God's people have been invited in every generation – to be transformed into a sign, foretaste and instrument of the kingdom (or reign) of God.[14]

- As sign, the Church points to the creating, loving, healing, just and forgiving God of the Scriptures, most clearly doing so in worship which marks it as a holy community of thanksgiving and praise.
- As foretaste, the Church embodies in its life the values of the reign of God, most clearly doing so in mutual love which marks it as a catholic (universal, all-inclusive) community of service.
- As instrument, the Church shares in God's mission in the world, most

clearly doing so in deeds and words which mark it as an apostolic community of witness.

The sent Church is marked by a unity built around the presence of the incarnate, crucified and risen Lord in its midst, whom it worships, serves and proclaims. Jesus, the Sent One of God, draws us to himself, breathes the Spirit upon us, and sends us out again in his name. As people of mission, we are nourished, renewed and transformed by Christ's presence among us. The spiritual life is, at its deepest levels, shaped by the God of mission.

In what ways is your church a sign pointing to the good news of God's reign in Christ? Or a foretaste of the community of God's redeemed people? Or an instrument for making the good news real and visible in your context?

The Five Marks of Mission

At its second meeting (Ely 1996), MISSIO began reviewing the 'Five Marks of Mission' as developed by the Anglican Consultative Council between 1984 and 1990. We recognize with gratitude that the Five Marks have won wide acceptance among Anglicans, and have given parishes and dioceses around the world a practical and memorable 'checklist' for mission activities.

However, we have come to believe that, as our Communion travels further along the road towards being mission-centred, the Five Marks need to be revisited.[15]

Mission: announcing good news

The first mark of mission, identified at ACC-6 with personal evangelism, is really a summary of what all mission is about, because it is based on Jesus' own summary of his mission (Matt. 4.17, Mark 1.14–15, Luke 4.18, Luke 7.22; cf. John 3.14–17). Instead of being just one (albeit the first) of five distinct activities, this should be the key statement about everything we do in mission.

Mission in context

All mission is done in a particular setting – the context. So, although there is a fundamental unity to the good news, it is shaped by the great diversity of places, times and cultures in which we live, proclaim and embody it. The Five Marks should not lead us to think that there are only five ways of doing mission!

The Five Marks of Mission
(ACC, 1984 and 1990)

The mission of the Church is the mission of Christ:

- To proclaim the good news of the kingdom of God.
- To teach, baptize and nurture new believers.
- To respond to human need by loving service.
- To seek to transform the unjust structures of society.
- To strive to safeguard the integrity of creation, and sustain and renew the life of the earth.

Mission as celebration and thanksgiving

An important feature of Anglicanism is our belief that worship is central to our common life. But worship is not just something we do alongside our witness to the good news: worship is itself a witness to the world. It is a sign that all of life is holy, that hope and meaning can be found in offering ourselves to God (cf. Rom. 12.1). And each time we celebrate the eucharist, we 'proclaim the Lord's death until he comes' (1 Cor. 11.26). Our liturgical life is a vital dimension of our mission calling; and although it is not included in the Five Marks, it undergirds the forms of public witness listed there.

Mission as Church

The Five Marks stress the doing of mission. Faithful action is the measure of our response to Christ (cf. Matt. 25.31–46; Jas 2.14–26). However, the challenge facing us is not just to do mission but to be a people of mission. That is, we are learning to allow every dimension of church life to be shaped and directed by our identity as a sign, foretaste and instrument of God's reign in Christ. Our understanding of mission needs to make that clear.

Mission as God-in-action

'Mission goes out from God. Mission is God's way of loving and saving the world ... So mission is never our invention or choice'

(Lambeth Conference 1998, Section II p. 121). The initiative in mission is God's, not ours. We are called simply to serve God's mission by living and proclaiming the good news. The Five Marks of Mission could make that clearer.

The Five Marks of Mission and beyond

We commend to each province (and its dioceses) the challenge of developing or revising its own understanding of mission which is faithful to Scripture. We suggest two possible ways forward.

- The Five Marks could be revised to take account of comments like those above. This has the advantage of retaining the familiar shape of the Five Marks.
- Alternatively a holistic statement of mission actions could be strengthened by setting out an understanding of the character of mission. This would affirm the solemn responsibility of each local church to discern how it will most faithfully serve God's mission in its context. An example of such an understanding is given below.

Mission is the creating, reconciling and transforming action of God, flowing from the community of love found in the Trinity, made known to all humanity in the person of Jesus, and entrusted to the faithful action and witness of the people of God who, in the power of the Spirit, are a sign, foretaste and instrument of the reign of God. (Adapted from a statement of the Commission on Mission of the National Council of Churches in Australia)

Whatever words or ideas each local expression of our Church uses, MISSIO hopes that they will be informed by three convictions:

- We are united by our commitment to serving the transforming mission of God.
- Mission is the bedrock of all we are, do and say as the people of God.
- Our faithfulness in mission will be expressed in a great diversity of mission models, strategies and practices.

If you were to ask people in leadership positions in your province (diocese, parish) whether they see mission as 'the bedrock of all we are, do and say as the people of God', how do you think they would answer?

Church Growth and Anglican Mission

In each of our four meetings, in four very different parts of the world, we have rejoiced to hear stories of the growth of the local church. We have ourselves seen communities faithfully worshipping, serving and proclaiming – sometimes in conditions of hardship, opposition, indifference or crushing poverty. We have been humbled by their courage and perseverance.

We have noted that among some Anglicans, 'growth' is often measured by the number of new parishes or dioceses that have been created. At times this emphasis gives the impression, perhaps unintentionally, that numbers are the primary criterion for growth. Numerical growth is often to be expected as one of the fruits of faithful witness. During our meeting in Zimbabwe we have experienced the wonder of worshipping with very large Anglican congregations whose music and dance has left us breathless.

However, to all who share our commitment to the mission of God, we offer two notes of concern about an undue emphasis on numbers (whether of people, parishes or dioceses) in assessing church growth.

- We hope that the emphasis on the number of new parishes or dioceses will be accompanied by attention to the quality of the growth that takes place. Church growth is also about such concerns as deepened commitment, spiritual maturity, more courageous discipleship, faithfulness in worship, service and witness.
- We hope that the emphasis on growth as 'church extension' – which has been a dominant model in the history of Anglican mission practice – does not veil a denominational imperialism. The mission of God is not about the triumphant spread of a particular church. Nor does creating more and more Anglican parishes necessarily fulfil it. Mission is the witness of the whole people of God to the good news made known in Christ. So we invite those of our provinces and mission agencies whose energies are enthusiastically given to church-planting to examine their approaches and priorities, and to seek ways to engage in the kind of mission which builds the unity of God's holy, universal and apostolic people, and so sets them free to engage with the world around them.

What understanding (or understandings) of 'growth' operate in your situation? If you were asked, 'In what ways is your church growing?' how would you answer the question?

Anglican Church Membership and Belonging

Belonging is a theme that MISSIO discerns as important in any discussion of mission. For example, the bishops in Section II of the 1998 Lambeth Conference heard about the Iona Community in Scotland, with its strong sense of ecumenical mission combined with a strongly incarnational spirituality. It seems to meet the need felt particularly among people in the West for intimacy, mutuality and personhood in community.[16]

Young people, in particular, are not attracted to traditional church membership. So the question arises: what kinds of belonging are appropriate in the Church? Is there only one kind of belonging?[17] Obviously a Church of mission needs to offer a sense of community and belonging, which is more satisfying and involving than institutional membership.

Both these illustrations find a basis in the important statement on unity adopted by the Seventh Assembly of the World Council of Churches (Canberra 1991). Titled 'The Unity of the Church as Koinonia: Gift and Calling', it challenges churches to take bold steps in partnership. Two issues arise for Anglicans. Are there limits to diversity? How do we maintain fellowship between those who cannot accept each other's views? While there are no easy answers, we are encouraged to be aware that the heart of *koinonia* or communion is life with the Father, through Christ, in the Spirit. This is the most profound communion possible for any of God's creatures.[18] Christians are bonded with God in 'a common mission witnessing to all people the Gospel of God's grace and serving the whole of creation'.[19]

We belong in God to one another. The challenge in mission is to bring others to experience this same quality of belonging or *koinonia*.

When people join an Anglican parish in your context, what kind of 'belonging' is offered? What procedures or structures do you have to help integrate new members into the *koinonia* (support, sharing, mutual care, solidarity) of the church?

The Church as Salt and Savour

There are some situations where Christian mission is conducted as if it were a military campaign, where conquest and victory are the dominant images of church growth. This leads some of MISSIO's members to wonder what it means to belong to the Church.

A member of MISSIO from Brazil reflects on this in the following way:

Many years ago (through the Crusades, the Inquisition, state proselytism, and so on) the church was occupied with baptizing people as the condition of membership and eternal salvation. Even today some churches hold campaigns or crusades to fill up their pews. This view sees the Church as a place to avoid eternal condemnation and to gain eternal happiness. In this perspective the growth of the Church is measured by the number of members, who are regarded almost as .'clients'. Being 'dough' is apparently more important than being 'leaven' (Matt. 13.33).

This is a temptation we need to resist. Adhering to God's plan is more important than just belonging to a church. Obeying God's call to justice and service is bigger than the issue of numbers in pews (cf. Isa. 65.14–21; Luke 4.17–25). The Church is no longer simply an ark of salvation, but God's agent of mission into the world. The liturgy should express, as a celebration, the action of my faith in transforming society, the Church and myself. So we need to recover the images of fermentation, of being salt, light, mustard seed. This is the true meaning of the catholicity of the Church. In addition to numbers, it is important to consider the commitment and the maturity of the church community, according to its context.

Instead of spending so much time domesticating new believers, the Church should remember its vocation to be a sign, foretaste and instrument of the mission of God. In this vision lay people, the people of the local congregation, are in the forefront. Church structures as well as the ordained ministry exist to prepare, animate and facilitate the quality of the Church's life, rather than simply looking enthusiastically for increased numbers of people. This ministry is called to be the means of empowering mission in order to transform the kingdoms of this world into the kingdom of God (cf. Rev. 11.15). The Christian community is a kind of task force to act for the transformation of world structures so that God's kingdom becomes a present gift here and now, in our history.

The key phrase in the Church now is 'fellowship-participation' rather than 'authority-obedience'. In this Church for the new millennium, we are invited not to succeed but to be obedient to Christ (John 20.21, Matt. 25.34ff).

So the vocation of the Church in our time is to work for the transformation of people and society. It is our opportunity to serve, celebrate and transform, as followers of Jesus. Our goal is not to harvest but to sow. We will be known by our fruits (Luke 6.44, Matt. 7.20–21) and God alone will judge.

Within this perspective, we may begin to understand the meaning of belonging to the Church. There are many kinds of belonging, and only God can judge them. Meanwhile, 'be merciful just as your Father is merciful' (Luke 6.36), because Christian faith is more akin to a new relationship than a religion (Matt. 25,1 John).[20]

What, in your experience, do parishes in your context emphasize more strongly: belonging to a community of fellowship and participation, or an institution of authority and obedience?

Companions in Mission

Elsewhere in this report we note the changes which have taken place in the patterns and structures of mission around the Anglican Communion over the past few decades. Here we wish to suggest that these changes – for example, the decreasing use of Partners-in-Mission consultations – give us the opportunity to reflect on the foundation of our relationships around the Communion. We suggest that the time has come to shift the focus in those relationships from partnership, which in many cases has taken on the flavour of a business relationship characterized by programmes and financial priorities, to companionship, which speaks of the priority of relationships, of sharing in solidarity.

We note in passing that a modified version of the ecumenical pattern of 'round table' conferences, which embodies many of the principles of the PIM process, offers a possible new way forward. Partners in such a model are not observers or commentators, but full participants. A pilot 'round table' conference is planned for Eastertide 2000 in the region covered by the South Pacific Anglican Council. This will go a step further than the former Partners-in-Mission consultation process.

> Review the partnership or companion relationships between your province (diocese, parish) and other parts of the Anglican Communion. What are the main features of the relationship? How much energy is given to the exchange of people and resources of mission and ministry? What place do financial matters have?

'Unreached Peoples'

MISSIO has, from its first meeting, had a concern for the question of evangelism among people who have never heard the gospel. However, we wish to stress that there are 'unreached peoples' in many different contexts, not just in those parts of the world which some describe as 'the 10/40 window'. There are such communities within many existing Anglican Provinces – including those in societies once thought to be 'Christian'.

We also wish to affirm that the prime responsibility for bringing the gospel to such communities lies with the nearest local church, rather than with missonaries from outside the context. Of course, the local church deserves support from the wider church, because we are all companions in the mission of God from everywhere to everywhere.

As Anglicans, we need to ensure that our witness among 'unreached peoples' is thoroughly incarnational, expressed through a presence which identifies with their culture and language, and through a proclamation which sensitively expresses the Christian faith in terms that they can hear and make their own. (See also the next two sections below, on 'Gospel, Church, Culture' and 'Christian Mission and Other Faiths'.) If a new Anglican church is planted in such a community, we will want to ensure that it is connected to the universal Church through episcopal ministry. The challenge MISSIO puts before each province of our Communion, then, is to identify areas where there is little or no Christian presence, to seek ways of engaging in mission ecumenically among them, and to discern the most appropriate shape of that mission.

What kinds of people or communities in your situation might be fairly dscribed as 'unreached'? What would be 'good news' for them?

Gospel, Church, Culture

Although there is undoubted truth and value in every spiritual and cultural tradition, this needs to be valued in the light of biblical teaching that all human beings are profoundly implicated in personal and corporate sin. There is, therefore, a need for discernment, so that we may be able to distinguish the good, the beautiful and the true, from the bad, the ugly and the false. For the Christian, God's saving acts, as they are recorded in the Scriptures, particularly his saving acts in Christ, provide the criteria necessary for the discernment.

... The truth in each tradition has 'attachment points' with the Gospel, so that when it is proclaimed in a particular culture, it can be understood and appropriated. It is in this way that the exercise of 'reason' has to be understood in our times. The Gospel has the capacity for becoming comprehensible to people of every intellectual tradition, world-view and spiritual belief.

... The Scriptures and the Fathers teach that it is God's will that all things should find their fulfilment (*anakephalaiosis*) in Christ (Eph. 1.10 and Irenaeus). This is particularly true of the authentic spiritual insights and aspirations of every culture and tradition.[21]

The 1996 Conference on World Mission and Evangelism in Salvador, Brazil[22] was a significant ecumenical event. Among the many themes it addressed, we welcome the conference's recognition that the relationship between the gospel and human culture is complex and dynamic. We need to appreciate that the gospel illuminates, challenges and transforms culture as much as culture illuminates and incarnates the gospel.[23]

In mission history the gospel has too often been identified with the culture of the missionary. The case study of the experience of

27

Anglicans in Canada, included in this report (chapter 7), makes this point vividly. Only in this century has our Communion begun to learn how to distinguish Anglo-Saxonism from Anglicanism. The gospel is not only a transforming challenge to human culture, but also to the Church itself. In the community of God's people, the gospel and culture intersect – and often clash. Wherever we are, wherever we incarnate God's mission – the sacramental presence of Jesus Christ – we need to be alive to the transforming work of the Spirit within us and among us, as well as in the world around us.

What is the experience of your province (diocese, parish) of the relationship between indigenous culture(s) and the gospel? How does the local church deal with tensions between the values of the gospel and the values of local culture?

Christian Mission and Other Faiths

The Section II report of the 1998 Lambeth Conference includes 30 theses on Christian responses to people of other faiths (p. 138). MISSIO sees no need to add to what is there, and commends it for study and action, along with the report of the Interfaith group. We include its resolution here for easy reference.

1998 Lambeth Conference
Resolution VI.1 – On Relations with People of Other Faiths
This Conference:

having heard about situations in different parts of the world where relations between people of different faiths vary from co-operation to conflict, believes that the approach of Christians to people of other faiths needs to be marked by:

i commitment to working towards genuinely open and loving human relationships, even in situations where co-existence seems impossible;

ii co-operation in addressing human concerns and working for justice, peace and reconciliation for the whole human community;

iii frank and honest exploration of both the common ground and the differences between the faiths;

iv prayerful and urgent action with all involved in tension and conflict, to understand their situation, so that everything possible may be done to tackle the causes of conflict;

v a desire both to listen to people of all faiths and to express our own deepest Christian beliefs, leaving the final outcome of our life and witness in the hands of God;

vi sharing and witnessing to all we know of the good news of Christ as our debt of love to all people whatever their religious affiliation.

recognises that by virtue of their engagement with people of other faiths in situations all over the world, Anglican Christians are in a special position to explore and develop genuinely Christian responses to these faiths;

also recognises that the Network for Inter-Faith Concerns (NIFCON) has been established by the ACC at the request of the last Lambeth Conference as a way for sharing news, information, ideas and resources relating to these concerns between provinces of the Anglican Communion;

recommends:

i that NIFCON be charged to monitor Muslim–Christian relations and report regularly to the Primates Meeting and the ACC;

ii that the ACC consider how to resource NIFCON adequately both in personnel and finance;

iii that all the other official Anglican networks should be encouraged to recognise the inter-faith dimensions to their work.

How does your province (diocese, parish) relate to people of other faiths? What are the points of co-operation or conflict? How might the ideas of the 1998 Lambeth Conference help you relate better to people of other faiths?

Mission and Anglican Identity

This is a large topic that lies outside MISSIO's primary agenda. However, questions do arise about whether there are distinctively Anglican ways of doing mission or evangelism, and whether

Anglican structures – such as the parish and diocese – help or hinder our mission endeavours. We encourage the widest possible study of those parts of Section II of the 1998 Lambeth Conference report, which deal with the missionary congregation and the missionary diocese.[24]

It is both possible and imperative that our ways of being Anglican – in our liturgies, our spiritualities, our parochial and diocesan structures, our interactions with the wider community – set us free to be transformed and transforming communities of mission. But this does not happen automatically. It demands a firm intention to examine all we are, do and say in the light of God's call to us to be united communities of holy worship, catholic ministry and apostolic mission.

This is sometimes easier to do at the level of the local parish, where the life of the Church is seen most concretely in communities of 'memory, meaning, celebration and hope'.[25] But, while the parish is wholly church, it is not the whole Church. As the 1998 Lambeth Conference said: 'While we are firm in our commitment to the local congregation, that does not make us congregational.'[26] The diocese has a key role to play in helping mission to happen in ways that are united, holy, catholic and apostolic.[27]

- The diocese can find opportunities for growth into unity, for example, by exercising joint responsibilities through face-to-face encounters that bring diverse parishes and other communities together.
- Dioceses need to encourage holiness by helping each parish to make spiritual transformation through worship a priority, and linking it to the exercise of worshippers' vocations in society.
- The catholic scope of the Church is made known through diocesan links between local parishes, with the province, the Communion and the wider Church. The diocese is often uniquely placed to raise the eyes of parishes beyond their own boundaries, and to encourage them to be more inclusive and diverse in their membership.
- The diocese can remind the parish of its apostolic charter and its fundamental call to mission in areas of both 'vitality and despair'.

How do your structures, procedures, relationships and use of resources promote or hinder your diocese's responsibility to build local churches which are united, holy, catholic and apostolic? Do your parishes experience the diocese as supportive and encouraging, or as demanding and draining of resources?

Conclusion

MISSIO offers these reflections, and the questions we have posed, as a resource to our sisters and brothers who lead us in the amazingly diverse contexts of mission and ministry which make up the Anglican Communion.

Our hope is that they will stimulate further reflection and action, so that, throughout our Communion, we may know the transforming presence of the God who has been revealed to us as the transforming community of the Sender, the Sent One, and the Strengthener of all who go.

4

Decade of Evangelism

Taste and see that the Lord is good;
Blessed is the man who takes refuge in him. (Psalm 34.8)

The Spirit of the Lord is on me,
because he has anointed me
to preach Good News to the poor . . . (Luke 4.18)

Introduction

The Decade of Evangelism has inevitably disturbed our Communion in the spheres where we felt a comfortable complacency. Many provinces, dioceses and churches responded positively to the call of the Decade as proposed by the Lambeth Conference 1988. Areas where the Church was already a vibrant reality appreciated the stimulation of new life around them. For some churches, seemingly rooted in a monotonous and repetitive model of Christianity, reflection and self-evaluation brought about a widened vision of the Anglican/Episcopal Church, and a new creativity as the power of God was made manifest.

This 200th decade of our era allowed us individually or corporately to begin to:

- Revitalize our churches in evangelism.
- Empower our laity and our clergy to embark on a vocation which has always been theirs.
- Recover an aspect of the Christian passion for the love of God for all of humankind.
- Be adventurous again in fields of failure where the missionary work was despised.
- Initiate and build new communities based on the biblical teachings.
- Sift the Church's values and install the contemporary reality in our expression of faith.
- Flavour our richness with a multitude of expressions that are culturally uplifting.

However diverse the effect of the Decade of Evangelism has been on the Communion, we are on our way to retrieving the essence of our vocation. We resonate to the words of Jesus, to be 'the salt of the earth and the light of the world'. And we recognize that there is much more to be done.

Background to the Decade

In 1988, the Lambeth Conference issued a rather modest call for a Decade of Evangelism. One could hardly imagine that much excitement could be ignited from the words of Resolution 43:

> This Conference, recognising that evangelism is the primary task given to the Church, asks each Province and diocese of the Anglican Communion, in co-operation with other Christians, to make the closing years of this millennium a 'Decade of Evangelism' with a renewed and united emphasis on making Christ known to the people of his world.

Ten years later, the Lambeth Conference called on the Church to build on what had been achieved by

> ... working for a transformed humanity, transformed cultures, a transformed mission for the Church, and transformed relationships with other Christian communities.

The boldness of the language, the breadth of the call, and the determination to carry the initiative forward all bear witness to the effectiveness of the Decade. Noting that during the Decade of Evangelism 'we have witnessed welcome changes in the world and enhanced efforts to share the Gospel of Christ', the conference declared nevertheless that 'many other injustices still disfigure our world and challenge our commitment to share the love of God' (Resolution V.4).

In 1988, in Resolution 44, the Lambeth Conference issued a call for 'a shift to a dynamic missionary emphasis going beyond care and nurture to proclamation and service', and therefore accepted 'the challenge this presents to diocesan and local church structures and patterns of worship and ministry'. Widespread acceptance of responsibility for the task – while also looking to God 'for a fresh movement of the Spirit' – has borne fruit. A preliminary analysis of a Communion-wide survey in 1998–99, and reflections from the

1995 mid-point review of the Decade, show widespread progress on this shift, and significant learnings. Paradoxically, the self-examination that usually has informed any effort to start or increase evangelistic efforts has led to recognition that yet more is required of the Church.

A Decade of Discovery

There is no doubt that the Decade of Evangelism, while not universally successful, has challenged many Anglicans to proclaim the gospel with renewed confidence. It has helped some to reclaim the very word 'evangelism'. It has attracted new members and created more vocations. It has mobilized dioceses and provinces to do more training, of different types. It has taught everyone that there are many models for evangelism. It has helped people deepen their spirituality and commitment to their communities. It has led people to rediscovering the Bible as the Word of God. Here is one account:

Church growth in Melanesia

The Church of Melanesia is 150 years old – and is the biggest church of the country. Come and gone are days when members of the Anglican Church have taken the faith for granted and the Church in Melanesia was stagnant.

The Decade of Evangelism rocked the church to spark new life. The gospel is proclaim, the parishes are becoming occupied with Bible studies and reaching out to others.

Young people are flowing into the four religious communities. The Society of St Francis, The Melanesian Brotherhood, the Sisters of the Church and the Sisters of Melanesia. So many have shown interest that the communities could hardly ever manage the numbers.

The religious communities have organized to do both primary evangelism and mission and evangelism. They plan their outreach with the parish priest and together subdivide the parish into zones so that every home in the parishes is visited and the gospel is shared. The brings about renewed life.

Primary evangelism is where the religious community members share a lot of their time with people, slowly trying to get the gospel through by understanding and living the life-style of the community concerned. This applies only to back-sliders and new converts.

Youth groups are becoming witnesses of the gospel and are reaching out with the message of the gospel to young people on the streets and villages throughout the province. They have shown great interest to do theological studies and be-coming part of the ordained ministry.

The Decade has caused the eight dioceses of the Province of Melanesia to establish training centres for lay workers of the church in order to equip them with the gospel and be part of the ministry. As a result, the parish churches are being ex-tended to cater for the growing numbers.

Under the leadership and direction of the Provincial Co-ordinator for Evangelism and Renewal and General Synod, the Church of Melanesia has produced study materials and courses for the Decade of Evangelism, set at three levels: intro-ductory, intermediate and advanced. The introductory course is for people in the parishes covering the basics of the Christian faith and Anglican traditions. It is also used in evangelism for those interested in the Christian faith. Inter-mediate and advanced courses are for discipleship, ministry, evangelism and leadership training. This has resulted in those who are trained, training others.

The Revd Canon Lionel Longarata
Melanesian Mission Board

Some other discoveries that Anglican evangelism leaders shared in the 1998–1999 survey are highlighted below.

People on the way

We have discovered that the churches in our Communion are on a pilgrimage, and the Decade has helped them to understand this. As the primates said in 1989 at their meeting in Cyprus, 'Approach the Decade of Evangelism not as a terminal point but as a begin-ning. We carry on the Decade as learners, expecting its end to be followed by decade after decade of evangelism. God's calling and sending forth are measured not by decades, but eternity.'[28]

The work of repentance

A major learning has to do with the necessity to repent and seek forgiveness of past sins before the work of evangelism can begin. How can you do evangelism without a clean record? The experience of Paul teaches us that with a cleansed heart and a transformed mind, one can move ahead. Nehemiah confesses on behalf of his people and himself: 'I confess the sins we Israelites, including myself and my father's house, have committed against you. We have acted very wickedly towards you. We have not obeyed the commands . . .' (Neh. 1.6–7).

During the Decade we have heard deeply moving testimonies, particularly from the Anglican Church of Canada and the Nippon Sei Ko Kai, of churches taking responsibility for past mistakes, apologizing on behalf of their people and church, and seeking forgiveness from those whom they have wronged (see appendix D). Although these churches may be small in membership, their powerful witness has pointed to an activity that is essential for transformation. Repentance before God and each other requires courage and humility, transparency and honesty. But once accomplished, there is release, freedom and new life. This, ultimately, is the message of the gospel.

During G-CODE, the mid-decade review conference in Kanuga, North Carolina, in 1995, the testimony of Bishop Joseph Iida of Japan and the subsequent acknowledgement and embrace from Colin Craston of England, 'sent waves of joy, repentance and reconciliation through the audience . . . later on many others apologised publicly to others and asked for forgiveness for national, ethnic and racial sins'.[29] This pattern has been repeated in many conferences and meetings since then, with cathartic results.

The blood of the martyrs

Anglicans have been reminded throughout the Decade of the courageous witness of their sisters and brothers suffering persecution under authoritarian regimes or violence, and atrocities perpetrated during civil conflict. Fear, famine and flight have been the reality for hundreds of thousands of Anglicans. Yet Sudan, particularly in the south, has seen people convert by the thousands during this decade. More than 2,000 songs of lament and faith, sorrow and triumph, have been composed – often by young women and men who have lived half their lives as refugees. The Communion can only stand in awe of such conviction, and give thanks for the witness of these souls.

Presenting the gospel

The Decade has encouraged us to take Jesus Christ to the people. We have been freed by the power of the Holy Spirit to act in the name of God: 'Hope does not disappoint us, because God has poured out his love into our hearts by the Holy Spirit whom he has given us' (Rom. 5.5). For Anglicans, known in some places as the 'frozen chosen', this is no small accomplishment.

> 'We have appointed a diocesan staff member to develop these areas and train people in them. Improvements and teaching in all these areas have had a positive effect on our diocese.' (An African diocese)

Reports gathered from all the provinces of the Communion show that people took initiative at every level of the Church – whether as individuals, congregations, dioceses or provinces. Provincial and diocesan co-ordinators of evangelism and mission have been appointed, and many parishes have named evangelism committees. Some new mission agencies have been created especially for the purpose of reaching the least evangelized peoples of the world.

Village ministry in Malaysia

Moon Hing is Vicar of St Peter's parish, a busy urban parish in Ipoh, the capital of Perak State, West Malaysia. His concerns reached beyond the parish boundaries to the villages of Malaysia, being challenged by what he had seen as a civil engineer working in villages in Malaysia and later in India. In 1993, with the blessing of the Diocesan Synod, Moon Hing and his wife, Sue Lan began Anglican Village Ministries (AVM).

'When I first came into this ministry,' said Moon Hing 'I had no clue of village life and thought it was just another urban set-up.' The cities reflected Malaysia's fast growing economy: new businesses, hospitals, schools, traffic jams, busy shops and markets. The villages lag years behind. The mining industry collapsed and the villagers were thrown into hard times. Young and active people left to find work in the towns or overseas; the less able-bodied, who were left behind, still struggle to make a living.

Moon Hing first worked in co-operation with 'Gospel to the Poor', an evangelical movement concerned with primary evangelism. As Gospel to the Poor moved on to other villages, AVM stayed behind to help new believers grow in their faith.

Leaving his successful business in Singapore and challenged by God's word to 'Seek first God's kingdom', Albert Tang returned to Malaysia to work with Gospel to the Poor in Mambang, a major village south of Ipoh. Albert had been baptized in St Peter's Church and encouraged by Moon Hing in his early Christian years. He later joined AVM when Gospel to the Poor moved on from Mambang. He became the first fulltime lay worker of AVM and his home in Mambang became a centre of worship, instruction and a base from which to travel to other villages. Later, Michael Yong with his wife Rebecca took the risk of selling their shop and joined AVM full-time, joining Albert in his ministry of prayer and worship meetings, Bible study and preparing people for the sacraments. In 1996 a group of people from Mambang were baptized in St Peter's Church. Two days later in their own village Bishop Lim of the Diocese of West Malaysia administered Confirmation to the new community.

The response to the gospel was greater than anticipated. Also the response was not from the more educated people, as expected, but from 'the old, the unemployed, the people who have really deep hurts and problems; they are the ones who respond because they see hope.' Moon Hing and Albert had to rethink their approach to the work. It became obvious that the gospel had to address physical as well as spiritual needs – care for the sick, work for the unemployed, in short, fulfil a desire to restore the fullness of human dignity to people. 'I want to qualify the word evangelism', said Moon Hing. 'It is not just the common understanding of telling someone about Jesus Christ. No. Evangelism is reaching the head, the heart, the body and everything. That's the evangelism we want.'

Moon Hing has a constant concern to keep mission on the agenda of city parishes and urges links between towns and villages sharing their resources, building relationships, praying together knowing that the Church is for everyone. 'We are moving into a new field which is quite lonely. There are no books, no training courses or manuals to tell us what to do. We have to design everything for ourselves.' But they are encouraged by those who have responded to the gospel, whose lives have been changed and have become witnesses of Christ to others.

(Condensed from *YES* magazine, Church Mission Society)

New life and worship

As people realized that Jesus Christ speaks to us today and every day, their lives were changed. This was true both for new Christians and for nominal Christians. In many parts of the Communion, women and men affirm that Jesus Christ is good news: he still heals, he still saves, he still gives people new life. As Anglicans declared or renewed their faith, they found themselves eager to share in lively worship. Young people especially brought contemporary ideas into the worship. As people claimed their faith, so they reclaimed their culture, bringing indigenous music and instruments into the worship. Indeed, more attention was given to every aspect of worship, so that in its excellence and relevance it might give the greater glory to God.

'Anglicans in Port Moresby became keen in reaching out to share their spiritual experiences with others, turning and winning souls for the expansion of God's kingdom.' (Church of the Province of Papua New Guiinea)

Transformed communities

In certain areas, transformed lives led to social action. The Archbishop of Canterbury reported that 'the Decade has helped begin to change the culture of the Church of England into one that is outward looking'.[30] People understood that the gospel had an important message for society, and involved themselves in justice issues. In Brazil, especially, the church is leading such initiatives.

> 'The "conversion agenda" is essential. Only those who are converted can evangelize and be sacrificial givers.' (Episcopal Church of the USA)

Teaching and training

With the enthusiastic response of people to the gospel, churches have realized that they need to equip individuals and groups for discipleship. Much effort has been expended on empowering the laity, women as well as men, youth in addition to older people. For some churches, this has meant utilizing previously untapped resources!

The story of Sabah: the development of a diocese

For the past 20 years, the strategy for the Interior Mission has been to train and use young evangelists. This training is done locally by our own priests and workers in the Bahasa Malay language. Materials from various sources are adapted to suit our own situation. We plan to continue this trend for the Interior Mission.

The Valley of Blessing Training Centre in Telupid is the main centre for training evangelists, teaching skills of personal witnessing to help the process of life changing in Jesus Christ. The Diocese of Sabah together with the Diocese of Singapore has developed a package of lay training materials. From our experience, we find that outreach and evangelism are the direct result of conversion. A person whose life is changed by Christ will naturally be concerned for the salvation of others.

As part of the strategy to challenge our diocese for evangelism and growth, the diocese decided on a theme for three years.

1991 Forward for ministries
The theme of the gifts of God to all believers in the Body of Christ was emphasized in all annual camps and conferences

for children, youth, women and men and church leaders. The challenge to our people (lay and ordained) was to share their gifts, for the enrichment of each other and for the building up of the body.

1992 Forward for growth

The emphasis in this year was spiritual growth (quality) and numerical growth (quantity).

1993 Forward for harvest

The emphasis was on training in the School of Evangelism in English, Chinese and Bahasa Malay. It was inspirational, skill-imparting and practical, including street witnessing, and all (including bishops and clergy) were commissioned and sent back to their own parishes/churches/mission districts to carry on with outreach and evangelism in their everyday life. The harvest was great.

This same year Mission 113 was initiated, each church member was challenged to reach one person with the gospel, every three years, and nurture that person to become a disciple. There was also an emphasis on obedience to God's Word at all levels of church life, knowing the fullness of God as Father, Son and Holy Spirit.

We have extended evangelism beyond the borders of Sabah to other countries in the Province of South East Asia. Short-term mission teams have been sent to our companion diocesan link, the Lichfield diocese in the UK. Other short-term mission team visits are planned for Mauritius, Perth, Sydney Australia and elsewhere.

In this decade the diocese has seen development and growth on every level. Growth has required the consecration of an assistant bishop, the appointment of a new archdeacon, ordination of new clergy and the empowering of laity for ministry. New parishes, training centres and programmes, projects to help the unemployed and new schools have been established. Even in the remote areas of Sabah the expectation and hope is that the churches will grow rapidly. The Anglican Christians are vibrant with life, energy and vision. Prayer, the Bible and obedience to the guidance of the Holy Spirit and practical training in evangelism and leadership are the forming factors of spirituality as we experience it. We will be making our critical evaluation of our progress in our next synod to be held at the end of August 1999. Please continue to pray for us.

The Most Revd Datuk Yong Ping Chung

There was a new drive to include evangelism and mission into the curricula of many seminaries and theological colleges. In the USA, representatives appointed by 11 deans meet annually as the Seminary Consultation on Mission to discuss progress in this regard. Theological education by extension grew, as did continuing education opportunities. Interestingly, Uganda's House of Bishops decided to abandon 'crash courses' (six months at Bible school) in favour of lengthier seminary training, recognizing that pastors required special leadership skills. In Sabah, there is a growing movement to do on-the-job training, sandwiching courses so as not to 'lock up' eager young persons for three or four years before they could answer God's call.

'The increase in the number of persons participating in our lay theological training programme is testimony to the awareness of the clergy and people alike of the necessity to have shared ministry engaged in God's mission in our Caribbean context.' (Church of the Province of West Indies)

Evangelism as a process

One thought emerging from the Decade is that evangelism takes place as a process. There have been many reports of the catechetical value of courses being offered by Alpha, Emmaus, Cursillo and local initiatives. These all provide a community group within which people can explore the Christian faith, often over a meal.

'Evangelism is a process with certain crystallizing moments along the way. Thus process and event work together.' (Church of England)

Egypt: 'Witness to Christ in society'

The Diocese of Egypt is large and varied stretching from Algeria, across North Africa and down to Ethiopia. The Church is small but is a constant witness in countries where most people regarded themselves as Muslim. Mission and evangelism in the Diocese of Egypt is to show God's love to the people, serving them through our institutions. The Joint Relief Ministry, Deaf Unit, social centres and Menouf School and Hospital continue to grow, and are strong areas of witness. The new appointment of an administrator who is skilled in management and ordained to the diaconate strengthens our unity of mission and the proclamation of the gospel by word and service. The Social Care Centre has recently been relocated, giving more space for growth in the work to aid the poor of Egypt.

The Episcopal Publishing House has seen growth during these past years and has a vision for further bookshops. A small bookshop was recently opened in the cathedral compound under the direction of the Episcopal Publishing House, and work is progressing on the Audio Visual Centre. Our aim is to reach more people of all ages with a message of Christ in a relevant way. The *Orient and Occident* magazine has taken new shape and is well produced by the enthusiastic new editor.

Cathedrals, places of worship and history are a silent witness to the Church in the past as well as the present day. There are pockets of growth in the Church: confirmations in St Luke's, Gambella, Ethiopia at one service numbered to 300. A new church was consecrated, Christ the King, and is held in a flat graciously provided by the Islamic Call Society. The Bishop of Egypt was invited to speak to 500 Islamic Call students on the Anglican Church. In recent years there has been steady growth in some of the congregations and encouragement of growth in the Arabic-speaking congregation in St Mark's with All Saints in Alexandria.

The Most Revd Ghais Malik

Multiplication and expansion

More people have meant more congregations, in certain regions at least, leading to the creation of new dioceses. Some provinces, such as Nigeria and Sudan, have experienced explosive growth. This caused Anglicans to recognize afresh the role that persecution and oppression plays in the growth of Christianity, especially in Islamic countries or under authoritarian regimes.

Nigeria: 'A province takes forward the decade'

The Anglican Church of Nigeria opened the Decade of Evangelism by consecrating nine new missionary bishops in the vast northern section of Africa's most populous nation.

The most Revd Joseph Abiodun Adetiloye, Archbishop of Nigeria, consecrated the new bishops on Sunday 29 April 1990 during a massive service in Abuja Cathedral. This was the beginning of the Archbishop's vision to provide an official Anglican presence in each state with an Anglican bishop who can be a spokesman for the Church on local governmental and societal issues. The new bishops are operating in a predominantly Muslim area where Muslim–Christian tensions have erupted over the years. The Church has seen phenomenal growth during this decade with 39 new dioceses having been formed, more than doubling the original number.

'It is God's time for the Church in Nigeria, a time of God's visitation (Acts 3)', said the Archbishop, in his introduction at the Church of Nigeria Forum at Lambeth 98 when he gave some reasons for the growth of the Church. The seed of the Word of God sown by his predecessors and the early missionaries is now bearing its reward. The missionary vision of the men and women, clergy and laity, God has given to today's Church in Nigeria. Taking risks in self-reliance, older dioceses supporting the new ones, empowering the laity as every baptized believer is in mission, a venture of partnership, the clergy as facilitators, catalysts and vision bearers. Every diocese appointed a co-ordinator for mission and evangelism.

In Nigeria no distinction is made between evangelism and

social action. The social needs are great and the Church is active in meeting the needs of poverty, education, health and training. Each diocese has their own programmes reaching out into the remote areas, many times pioneering through great difficulties and hardship.

The Church of Nigeria Missionary Society (CNMS) was founded in 1997 and now boasts 11 missionaries, both lay and ordained, men and women, and all university graduates. After a period of training they were sent out to work among 'unreached', often nomadic peoples in remote parts of Nigeria. Blessing Nwigwe is one example whose work is primary evangelism and social action in the completely unreached area of Kebbi's nomadic peoples, an area hardly anyone knew existed. CNMS is looking at neighbouring countries like Chad and Burkina Faso and hopes to go international in three or four years time when it has gained more experience of missionary work in Nigeria.

The growth of the Church and the increased number of dioceses to cope with the growth brought about another major move forward for the Church in Nigeria. The Archbishop declared in his sermon at the Standing Committee Meeting in Owerri on 27 April 1997 that the Church decided to create three provinces within the Church of Nigeria with three archbishops under one primate.

Archbishop Adetiloye concluded his sermon, 'The challenge that faces the Church in Nigeria today is the need for social transformation, development and leadership training and for the church to become God's voice and servant for the redemption of society as well as example and pattern of leadership of the salvation of the nation and people.'

(Excerpts from reports and sermons from Nigeria)

However, exciting new growth has brought new challenges – the need for more churches, more trained leaders, and finances to meet the demands. The need for salaries, housing, church buildings, vehicles, and other equipment puts tremendous pressure on the leadership of the Church.

> 'We have started over ten parishes in the past decade, and we are looking at starting one or two dioceses in the near future. We are very keen in our endeavours.' (Hong Kong Sheng Kung Hui)

Stewardship

There is evidence that new enthusiasm about the Church has led people to increase their giving of time, talent and treasure. In places, new teaching and commitment have led to increased tithing. People seem to have a clearer understanding of the role they all play in the Christian community and the work of the gospel. They give more time to prayer, Bible study, meetings, outreach, and visiting – all in all, sharing more deeply in the life of discipleship.

> 'In 1994 we embarked as a diocese on the RENEW process, which has helped many parishes to grow and become financially viable. The foundations are laid for mission as we enter the new millennium.' (Diocese of Klerksdorp, Church of the Province of Southern Africa)

New relationships

A number of events throughout the Decade have brought people together, leading to new friendships as well as new understandings. Visiting and networking has increased at provincial, diocesan and individual parish levels. This has led to a broadened sharing of gifts, a sharing of the rich diversity of Anglicanism. The bonds of affection that distinguish our Communion have been strengthened, despite differences of opinion on certain social issues.

> 'We have learned the importance of being outward-looking rather than inward, proactive rather than reactive.' (Diocese of Bendigo, Anglican Church of Australia)

A new unity

Many have discovered that the work of evangelism means not only crossing boundaries, but also building bridges. Within the Church, working to spread the good news has helped bring Anglicans together. People have learned that different situations require different models, and that all are complementary to fulfilling God's mission.

All is grace: A story from Brazil

Perhaps because the Anglican Church in Brazil is so small, many people are worried about statistics. The Church's action is summed up in the number of baptized or confirmed members. They forget that God's Spirit works beyond the walls of the church. We could spend hours speaking of the grace of God in the world.

I would just like to cite a recent story; an important leader in our community, despite being Roman Catholic, asked us to bless his house. He believed that he needed a greater presence of God in his home as his wife was ill and suffering from depression. Ruth and I went one evening to his home to attend to his request. When we arrived, there was a small group of people there who lived nearby. We gave the family a candlestick and candle, blessed during the liturgy, which is now in an important place in the entrance of the home. A few days later we met him again. He was very pleased with the recuperation of his wife who was finally free from depression. He was very grateful because he knew that the healing of his wife was due to the result of the grace of God! This couple will probably never become Anglican, and this event will not appear on our statistics, but it was a true experience of the grace of God acting in his life. All is grace!

We are coming to the beginning of a new Christian millennium. This has made many churches reflect on their mission and their message. Are we really proclaiming the gospel? Or are we simply concerned with statistics?

The Revd Meriglei
Diocese of South Western Brazil

This is not only an Anglican matter: there are reports of improved ecumenical relationships or ecumenical evangelistic ventures as well. The remarkable new enthusiasm of Anglicans sparked other Christian communities to evangelism initiatives of their own. In fact, churches occasionally worked together in planning evangelistic campaigns.

> 'Within our own region, we will be considering new initiatives in urban evangelism, inter-diocesan co-operation in "frontier areas", youth evangelism, cross-cultural evangelism, and church growth among indigenous communities. As a contribution outside the Southern Cone, we have accepted an invitation from the Iglesia España Reformada Episcopal to send an evangelistic team to Spain in the year 2000.' (Iglesia Anglicana del Cono Sur de America)

In Uganda, for example, the Pentecostal Churches had previously called the Anglican Church a 'dead' church and urged people to abandon it. Thus, they increased their own following. But with the advent of the Decade of Evangelism and the fire of the Holy Spirit that came with it, many were drawn back into the Anglican Church. The Pentecostals stopped preaching against the Anglicans, and began to work with them to preach the gospel.

The Anglican Communion Office and the Decade

Although the Decade of Evangelism was meant to involve every entity within the Anglican Communion, responsibility was given to the Anglican Communion Office in London to carry out various preparatory and programmatic exercises.

The time from the 1988 Lambeth Conference to the launching of the Decade in January 1991 was designated as a time of planning and preparation. Lambeth referred the Decade to the ACC, and ACC referred it to MISAG II. The Revd Martin Mbwana, then Director of Mission and Social Issues, was staff to the group but sadly fell terminally ill. The primates, meeting in Cyprus in 1989, offered very useful guidelines for the Decade and urged provinces to gather statements, stories, strategies, and experiences for sharing. They also requested all dioceses, parishes and religious communities to engage in prayer for the Decade.

The Revd Canon Dr Robert W. Renouf was seconded to the Anglican Communion Office from the Episcopal Church in the USA, to serve as adviser to the Decade, beginning in 1989. A logo for the Decade was created, and the office began soliciting original prayers from throughout the Communion. These were published in a series of prayer cards and mailed out to 400 Anglican religious communities and orders; all primates, bishops, and provincial secretaries; theological colleges, seminaries and schools; mission agencies, and subscribers to *Anglican Information*.

Also circulated with the prayer cards was a newsletter, *Sharings*, offering stories, strategies, statements and experiences in evangelism from around the Communion. Work began on the video, 'On the Move with Christ', under the direction of the Revd Dr Robert T. Browne of the USA, showing mission and evangelism being practised throughout the Communion. Dr Browne subsequently produced another marvellous tool for the Communion, called 'The Many Faces of Anglicanism'.

Meanwhile, ACC-8 and the leadership of the Communion generally, were urged to reflect on the reports of MISAG I and MISAG II (*Giving Mission its Proper Place* and *Renew Our Vision in Mission*, respectively) as well as the report of the Mission and Ministry Section of the 1988 Lambeth Conference, entitled *The Truth Shall Make You Free*. The ACC offered assistance and encouragement to the provinces in the preparatory phase.

In 1991, MISAG II published *Renew Our Vision in Evangelism: A Study Guide for the Decade of Evangelism*. It offered stories from throughout the Communion, with scripture passages and discussion questions, to help people reflect. Another book, *By Word and Deed: Sharing the Good News through Mission*, was well under way, with various authors offering contextual models for evangelism and mission.

The Decade office reported that the list of print, audio-visual and people resources was growing, and a directory of religious orders and communities was being prepared. In a status report for the joint meeting of the primates and the ACC standing committees in 1991, Canon Renouf noted that the provinces had been surveyed and a major problem had been identified – 'the need for mission training of laity and clergy ... and the development of organizational structures and strategies to support the major shift to mission'. The survey of MISAG II to theological students and colleges also revealed the need to include mission and evangelism training in the curriculum.

That year, the ACC appointed the Revd Canon Dr Cyril Okorocha as Director of Mission and Evangelism for the Anglican Communion. He soon embarked on an extensive travel programme, accepting invitations from provinces and dioceses to speak, teach, and preach. He participated in launching Decade programmes at provincial and diocesan levels, facilitated training programmes in mission and evangelism for clergy and lay people, helped organize a variety of meetings and conferences, and generally sought to animate evangelism campaigns throughout the Communion.

In 1993, the joint standing committees meeting in Cape Town accepted the MISAG II recommendation that the Anglican Communion have a standing commission on mission and evangelism. They named it MISSIO and asked the primates to appoint regional representatives. The first meeting was held in November 1994. One of the many tasks MISSIO was given by the primates, the joint standing committees, and the Anglican Consultative Council, was the responsibility to track the Decade. Through its members and the various consultants and staff of the Anglican Communion Office, MISSIO has encouraged, resourced, and monitored the effort in a variety of ways.

Meanwhile, Dr Okorocha was working with an extensive international team to organize the mid-decade review of evangelism requested by ACC-9. Named 'Global Conference on Dynamic Evangelism Beyond 2000' (G-CODE 2000), this important conference was held in Kanuga, North Carolina, USA in September 1995. Its key findings are included in appendix B.

After the conference, Dr Okorocha gathered the rich input into a book called, *The Cutting Edge of Mission*. The stirring speeches, regional presentations, group reports, resolutions and other findings are all there. But the joyful nature of the event can only be glimpsed. The primary lesson of the event was the importance of being together. It was the largest and most diverse gathering of Anglicans since the Toronto Congress in 1963, and strengthened the conviction of many that the model of large gatherings is worth continuing.

The conference was meant to evaluate progress in the movement from maintenance to mission, but it also gave new impetus to the Decade. There was a surge of activity throughout the Communion, resulting from general inspiration, new relationships, and spiritual strengthening.

The two South-to-South conferences deserve mention, because they occurred during the Decade, occupied a great deal of time and energy in the mission and evangelism office, and undoubtedly influenced the activities and achievements being discussed. They had their roots in work done by the Mission Agencies Working Group and the Mission Issues and Strategy Advisory Group, and were carried forward by MISSIO. The first Anglican Encounter in the South took place in Nairobi in January 1994; the second in Kuala Lumpur in February 1997. Evangelism, mission, and the role and interpretation of Scripture were key topics at both. These gatherings of Anglicans from the Two-Thirds World have had an important impact on the Communion. The statements issued from both conferences, 'Trumpets from the South', were wake-up calls from the regions where Anglicanism is growing most rapidly.

Dr Okorocha's contract expired at the end of 1997. The joint standing committees recommended that the outcomes of the Lambeth Conference be evaluated, and the overall priorities of the Anglican Communion Office be assessed, before any new staff members were chosen.

During 1998 and 1999, Miss Marjorie Murphy, secretary for the office for the past 11 years, has continued to gather resources, track activities, keep in touch with mission and evangelism co-ordinators, and respond to requests for information. During the same time period, another survey of the provinces has been conducted in an attempt to evaluate achievements, lessons learned, challenges for the future.

The following questions were included in the survey:

- Give examples of ways the challenge to 'shift from maintenance to mission' has affected your province/diocese.
- What are the major factors influencing the success/failure/indifference of the Decade in a given situation?

- What are the most important lessons learned in your province/diocese during the Decade?
- What changes, if any, are planned (present and future) in the training of clergy/laity for the mission of the Church?
- What steps is your province/diocese planning for mission and evangelism as we move into the next millennium?

The survey responses continue to be received and collated in the mission and evangelism office, and will be available from there. Analysis of this raw material is an important next step for the next Mission Commission.

Throughout the Decade, prayers have been gathered from every part of the Communion. Publication of these would provide rich blessing for all Anglicans, and MISSIO recommends that this be done. Resource lists have been expanded, including Internet websites, and a list of people-skills available throughout the Communion has reached impressive proportions. Thanks for all this work go to Marjorie Murphy, who also maintains the list of known provincial and diocesan mission and evangelism co-ordinators.

In summary, the mission and evangelism staff assisted the Anglican Communion Office as it implemented the initiatives of the various official structures of the Communion – namely, the Anglican Consultative Council, the primates, the joint standing committees, and the Lambeth Conference. For all these bodies, the proclamation of a Decade of Evangelism provided the obligation to keep the goals ever before us.

The Way Forward

At the time of MISSIO's final meeting, the Decade of Evangelism was still in progress. Many voices from around the Communion say that the Decade has added great momentum to the on-going witness of Anglicans worldwide which will continue beyond the official end of the Decade.

Although not in a position to make a definitive assessment of the impact of the Decade of Evangelism, MISSIO does make some suggestions arising from its preliminary evaluation. Some trends are clear, and some common themes deserve further reflection or action. In time, we believe, it would be valuable to do a comprehensive analysis of the ways in which the Decade of Evangelism has (or has not) been received and implemented in the very diverse parts of our Communion. We recommend that this task be undertaken by the staff of the Anglican Communion Office over the next two or three years.

Suggestions

- Throughout the Communion, keep the evangelism momentum in high profile in the Church's mission, from the primates' meeting to the ACC and all synodical structures.
- Help the Anglican Communion Office keep its list of potential resources up to date.
- Urge the appointment of a full-time, senior-level mission and evangelism staff person in the Anglican Communion Office to provide leadership and co-ordinate communication among the provinces.
- Continue leadership training of both men and women for effective work in mission and evangelism.
- Encourage provinces and dioceses to make the best use of their internal resources, and not look only for external resources to carry out programmes.
- Revive and strengthen the catechumenal process in congregations and small groups. The Diocese of Sabah reports its most dramatic growth in those parishes using the cell church model, where 'dynamic, enabling groups of 10 or 15 become caring, evangelistic groups'.
- Affirm the effective utilization of every culture in the process of evangelism, whether in local congregations or internationally, throughout the Communion.
- Keep a clear focus on the Triune God, so as not to be trapped in a shallow proclamation. Emphasizing only one aspect of the Trinity will limit people's understanding of the gospel and thus will inhibit transformation.
- Stand with and encourage the persecuted churches and those torn by wars, where proclamation is not allowed and evangelism is forbidden by the nation. Continually apply great caution and sensitivity with regard to such situations.
- In the words of Raymond Fung, consultant to the 1995 G-CODE conference: 'Don't marginalise evangelism ... Don't overload it ... Don't domesticate it ... Articulate it!'[31]

Recommendations

Two major areas of the impact of the Decade expressed throughout the Communion were: the added momentum to the witness of the Church – the shift from maintenance to mission is already evident in the churches around the Communion; and secondly the increase of the number of persons participating in mission and evangelism training as well as in theology both among the lay people and the clergy. MISSIO recommends therefore:

- That the provinces and dioceses of the Communion evaluate the lessons learnt during the Decade in their situation in order to continue and build on the momentum the Decade has achieved and to keep evangelism as a high profile in the Church's mission.
- That in particular the provinces, dioceses and parishes develop and expand appropriate training to equip individuals and congregations for effective work in mission and evangelism.

Questions for Reflection and Discussion

- How did your province (diocese, parish, agency) respond to the call for a Decade of Evangelism? What factors shaped that response (e.g. past experiences of evangelism, your socio-political context, your church's identity or ethos)?
- How did your province (diocese, parish, agency) understand 'evangelism' at the start of the Decade? Has it changed since then? If so, in what ways?
- How do you see evangelism relating to the wider task of mission, as this report has expressed it? (See *The Five Marks of Mission*, pp. 18–20).
- Who, in your context, have been (or are now) the primary agents of evangelism?
- What forms of training (if any) in evangelism have been offered in your setting? What was found to be effective, and what was less helpful?
- To what extent has the Decade of Evangelism had an impact on other dimensions of local church life, such as worship, patterns of ministry, theological education, or social action?
- What was the role of the province or the dioceses in guiding, shaping and resourcing parishes for evangelism? Could this role have been improved? If so, how?
- What styles or practices of evangelism did you find most effective in your context? (Examples might be friendship evangelism, revival services, house groups, neighbourhood visiting, large rallies, ecumenical ventures, liturgical evangelism, enquirers' groups, catechumenal groups, using the mass media and publications.) How might you build on them?
- If you were to start the Decade of Evangelism again, what would you do differently? What would you do the same?
- Networks of people with common interests strengthen all aspects of the Church, international as well as local. Do we help or hinder such voluntary associations in our regions?

- Do we cultivate a spirit of welcome and invitation in our churches? Churches that are perceived to be genuine will draw people who are seeking God into their fold, and will become companions to them on the journey of faith.
- The Anglican Communion affirms that it is a comprehensive church. Do we celebrate the rich diversity of our Christian community? Have we isolated ourselves from our neighbours? Or are we open to receiving those who are different from us?

5

Training Leadership for Mission

Introduction

Christ chose some of us to be apostles, prophets, missionaries, pastors and teachers, so that his people would learn to serve and his Body would grow strong. This will continue until we are united by our faith and by our understanding of the Son of God. Then we will be mature, just as Christ is, and we will be completely like him. (Eph. 4.11–13 Contemporary English Version)

The issue of equipping the ordained and lay leadership of the Anglican Church for ministry and mission was raised many times during the Decade of Evangelism and before that at the 1988 Lambeth Conference.[32] The Report of the Mid-Decade Review Conference in Kanuga contained major sections on: the ministry of the whole Church, the ministry of laity in the world and in the Church, empowering the whole people of God for his mission and ministry, a theology of lay ministry, the ordained ministry.[33] These headings indicated the complexity of the issues involved.

The survey which was sent to provinces after the mid-point review of the Decade of Evangelism Conference at Kanuga, North Carolina asked the question, 'What changes, if any, are planned (present and future) in the training of clergy/laity for mission of the Church?'

The West Indies response was representative: mission must shape our ecclesiology and the objectives of training for ordained and lay ministry. Indeed there must be mutual and collaborative ministry, inspired and motivated by a common sense of participation in God's mission. This way is the way forward.

The report of the Second Mission Issues and Strategy Advisory

Group (MISAG II) states: 'Effectiveness in mission depends upon the whole people of God being adequately equipped and trained for the task whatever their sphere of involvement. Theological education therefore is of fundamental importance for this process of equipping the people of God for their mission and ministry in the world.'[34]

The same report also stated that to be relevant to life and to meet people's needs, theological education must address issues that concern all aspects of everyday life and worship – spiritual, social and material. Today, leadership training for mission is needed for both laity and clergy, and such training needs to be relevant to the lives of Anglicans currently in extraordinary situations such as war (Congo, Sudan, Papua New Guinea), oppression and flight (Rwandan and Sudanese refugees), and famine (parts of Tanzania). Anglicans in these contexts are doing theological education as they worship and witness to their hope in God in horrific circumstances.

The Aims of Training Leadership for Mission

In the context of a Church being transformed for mission, the aims of leadership training need to include the following:

- To equip all the people of God for mission and ministry.
- To enable them to become mature in Christ through spiritual and ministerial formation.
- To help them develop willingness to listen and observe, so that they may come to an intelligent understanding of the signs of God in their lives, in the community, in the context in which they live and in the world.
- To develop skills in social and contextual analysis.
- To encourage prophetic voices and courageous stances.

One example of such training is Bishopdale College in the Diocese of Nelson, New Zealand, where laity, ordinands and clergy train together for a diploma in ministry. They also meet together for regional ministry training, to acquire skills in practical ministry skills over a five-year period. Another example is the School of Evangelism for the Interior Mission at Telufid in the Diocese of Sabah, Malaysia. The school trains leaders for cross-cultural mission and evangelism.

The Sabah example

For the past 20 years, the strategy for the Interior Mission has been to train and use young evangelists. This training is done locally by our own priests and workers in the Bahasa Malaysia language. Materials from various sources are adapted to suit our own situation. We plan to continue this trend for the Interior Mission.

Training Ordained Leadership

Provinces and dioceses need to assess the curricula of their seminaries and other training institutions (including extension and in-service programmes) to ensure that they reflect a central concern for the mission of God. Curricula need to include specific missiological courses, but also, other subjects need to have missiological perspectives applied to them. For example, church history and pastoral care need to be informed by missiological perspectives. Biblical studies, too, need to be taught in the same way. The Scriptures are missionary texts and need to be seen as the story of a missionary God. Paul's letters, for example, were written on the road to communities formed in mission and being formed for mission. In Martin Kaehler's words, 'mission is the mother of all theology.'

Residential theological colleges, theological education by extension programmes and in-service models are all widely used around the Anglican Communion. A good example of the in-service model is the training of Maori priests in New Zealand. The five regions all have short winter and summer sessions, as most of the priests are non-stipendiary and have secular occupations.

Training Lay Leadership

Christian formation and nurture is basic mission work. In every cultural context Christians live on a mission frontier and need training to lead formation processes such as the catechumenate, the Alpha and Emmaus courses (introductory group study courses on Christian faith), nurture groups and cell groups, all of which play a fundamental role in equipping people for their Christian life and witness. A list of formation courses that have been used around the Communion during the Decade of Evangelism is available from the Anglican Communion Office, mission and evangelism desk.

Cross-cultural encounters are important as a part of Christian formation. There is a need for people in training to have opportunities to exchange experiences and insights between different parts of the world. The team visits between the Dioceses of Lichfield, Sabah, West Malaysia, Kuching, and Qu'Appelle are an example of this. Another example is the Canadian programme enabling theological students to do a three- or four-month internship in another part of the Communion.

Our dialogue with people of different faiths must be taken seriously, always remembering those who may be suffering from religious persecution where dialogue has been overtaken by hatred and violence. Sudan, India, the Arab world and Indonesia have provided examples of this recently. The training of lay leaders takes place in diverse cultures and contexts throughout our Communion and needs to prepare people for diverse forms of ministry including sharing their faith in appropriate ways.

In many of the growing churches of Africa lay catechists and evangelists need to be trained to take responsibility for congregations under an ordained person who may be able to visit the congregation only a few times a year.

Questions for Reflection and Discussion

- What models does your church use for training lay and ordained leadership?
- How do you train people who have specific gifts for mission and evangelism?
- What resources are available in your area to equip Anglicans for cross-cultural mission?
- What are the strengths and weaknesses of this training in your province?
- What input does your church leadership have on theological curricula?
- Does your continuing education programme inspire and refresh your bishops, clergy and lay leaders?

A story from Brazil

A son told his father that he didn't want to go to church one Sunday. The father asked for three sensible reasons to justify his position! The son replied, 'The servers are lazy; the music is boring; the congregation is so complicated; I am fed up.' Then the father patiently replied with three reasons which would justify a change in the attitude of the son, and said, 'My son, the church needs you; you are 40 years old; and you are the parish priest!'

Recommendation

MISSIO, recognizing that its surveys of the progress of the Decade of Evangelism within dioceses and provinces have highlighted the importance and problems of leadership training and clergy formation, therefore requests ACC-11 to initiate a review within the Communion of leadership training and clergy formation to identify trends, needs and problems, and how they might be addressed.

6

Patterns of International Mission Structures in the Anglican Communion

Introduction

The intention of this chapter is to outline the development of structures and connections for international mission within the Anglican Communion and the principles that underlie them. It also includes examples of recent expressions of cross-cultural mission, and concludes with proposals for the next stage in Anglican Communion international mission structures. The chapter does not consider internal mission within provinces, but it does raise the question of how best to bring together internal and international mission.

The Role and Purpose of Structures

A structure is the way a group organizes itself for particular tasks, functions or purposes. Its success can be assessed by its effectiveness in accomplishing its tasks. A structure should change and develop as its purposes change. Structures can be experienced both negatively and positively. Negatively, a structure can be heavy, controlling, bureaucratic, committee-bound and too rigid or hierarchical for an organization's purpose. It can dominate and be unjust. Positively, a structure can be enabling, invigorating, flexible and collaborative, allowing space for initiative and creative development. The tests for any structure are the extent to which it is life-giving and energizing, and its effectiveness in achieving its functions.

In assessing structures for international mission in an Anglican Communion of autonomous provinces and independent agencies, we are looking for structures that are light, flexible, responsive, collaborative, easy to manage, facilitating connections. The purpose of the connections is to foster relationships between provinces, their dioceses and mission agencies, so as to improve the appropriate mission response to the different contexts in which the churches of the Communion are set. The structure should enable relationships to develop and so permit the great variety of mission challenges and responses across the Communion to inform, encourage, support, challenge and critique each other. It should allow space for initiatives and those surprises so characteristic of the work of God's Spirit. Indeed, all structures of the Anglican Communion should be evaluated according to their contribution to the work of the Church in serving the mission of God.

Some Underlying Principles

In any discussion of structures for mission within the Anglican Communion, one must remember that the primary responsibility for worship and witness in each place lies with the Christians who are there. They are the local expression of the universal Church. Most Anglican Christians are part of a parish, which may consist of one or more congregations. But the parish is not on its own. It is part of a diocese in which the bishop shares responsibility for the care of souls with the clergy. Although the diocese is the basic unit of Anglicanism, dioceses themselves are connected together into provinces.

For most Christians, mission and witness take place in the local community and in the place of work, through the natural every-day process of living, working and relating with others. But special activities and programmes also supplement the daily life and witness of Christian people. These may be organized by church bodies or by voluntary movements. The corporate struc-tures of the Church are the congregations, dioceses and provinces, their councils and synods. Such special activities may have to do with the formation of new churches, education, healing, social action for justice and development, relations with government and campaigning on particular issues. They are an expression of the collective witness of a Church responding to the context in which it is set.

Voluntary movements are an important way in which Chris-tians have expressed their commitment to a particular task. The religious orders and the missionary societies are notable expressions of the voluntary principle (the right of Christians to associate together to fulfil a particular objective).

A theological framework for this mix of structures for worship, service and witness is to see the Church as a movement, the pilgrim people of God journeying to the kingdom. Within this large movement, there arise many smaller movements as faithful Christians seek, under the Spirit, to fulfil their vocations in a variety of ways. Such movements may be about evangelization, issues of justice and peace, advocacy for the powerless.

The role of church leadership in relation to such movements is to provide recognition, facilitation and direction, but not control. Bishops, as those whose office is the focus of the unity, catholicity and mission of the Church, need to ensure that there are adequate structures within their dioceses and provinces for representatives of such movements to meet with representatives of the Church's leadership for consultation, co-ordination and planning.

A voluntary movement within the Church should be close enough to the Church's structures and leaders, and yet true enough to its own task, to be a genuine resource and witness to the Church.

Mutual Responsibility and Interdependence

The rapid growth of the Church in Africa, Asia and Latin America and the formation of new autonomous provinces have contributed to the multiplicity of mission experiences and the need to find ways to connect in order to provide mutual encouragement, support and challenge. Since 1963 the Anglican Communion has initiated two Communion-wide programmes to encourage mutual participation and support in the mission of the Church – Mutual Responsibility and Interdependence (MRI) and Partners in Mission (PIM).

The Communion as a whole began its journey from paternalism to partnership in its mission relations in the 1960s. In 1963, just prior to the Anglican Congress in Toronto, the primates and metropolitans of the Communion issued a 'manifesto', 'Mutual Responsibility and Interdependence in the Body of Christ' – MRI. Their proposal was essentially to look at needs (for people, finance, skills and infrastructure) across the Communion and to

gather and distribute resources to meet those needs. It was a challenge to break out of the donor/recipient mindset of the colonial
era and move into new relationships of equality and mutuality,
not just in financial sharing but in personnel and other aspects of
Christian discipleship. A call was made for a fund of £5 million to
assist the new provinces. A priority was theological education to
encourage self-reliance in leadership. MRI increased awareness
of the Communion, the need for partnership, and the principles
on which it should be based. The final part of the manifesto reads
as follows:

> We are aware that such a programme as we propose, if it is
> seen in its true size and accepted, will mean the death of
> much that is familiar about our churches now. It will mean
> radical change in our priorities – even leading us to share
> with others as much as we spend on ourselves. It means the
> death of old isolations and inherited attitudes. It means a will-
> ingness to forgo many desirable things, in every church.

> In substance what we are really asking is the rebirth of the
> Anglican Communion, which means the death of many old
> things but – infinitely more – the birth of entirely new
> relationships. We regard this as the essential task before the
> churches of the Anglican Communion now.[35]

The vision was inspiring and in keeping with independence movements sweeping colonial parts of the world. However, changing
behaviour is a different story from seeing visions and dreaming
dreams. The Anglican Communion's Executive Officer in
London and his regional representatives implemented the vision
of MRI through a 'Directory of Projects'. The focus on money
contributed to a 'shopping list mentality' in which churches of the
South or Third World prepared lists of projects which the churches
of the North or First World, agreed to fund ... or not. Personnel
needs were more difficult to meet. Somehow the balance of power
did not shift sufficiently to enable full relationships of mutuality
and interdependence. Those who controlled the purse strings still
held most of the power. Nevertheless MRI was a most significant
initiative in propelling the Communion along the path to greater
mutuality.

One of its fruits was the encouragement of companion diocese links (which had begun from the USA in the 1950s) as a means of enabling the exchange of prayer, information and encounter through face-to-face meeting across the Communion.

Partners-in-Mission

A second development was the Partners-in-Mission process. This emerged because of the difficulties associated with MRI, and attempted to foster a wider interpretation of partnership. The principles for PIM were stated at the first two ACC Meetings in Limuru (1971) and particularly Dublin (1973). They remain of abiding importance for the Communion and bear repeating.

> The responsibility for mission in any place belongs primarily to the church in that place. However, the universality of the Gospel and the oneness of God's mission mean also that this mission must be shared in each and every place with fellow-Christians from each and every part of the world with their distinctive insights and contributions. If we once acted as though there were only givers who had nothing to receive and receivers who had nothing to give, the oneness of the mission-ary task must now make us all both givers and receivers.[36]

In place of the 'Directory' system a new vehicle was proposed. Each church was to engage in a planning process to set its own mission priorities. This process was to be undertaken with the active participation of partner churches, selected by the host. The Partners-in-Mission, or PIM, process was born.

Developing Communion-wide programmes in a voluntary association of autonomous dioceses is not easy. But provinces agreed to a programme of consultations to which representatives of partner Anglican and other Churches would be invited to assist them in setting their mission priorities and assessing the help they would need from others. A detailed programme of consultations was worked out for the 1970s and early 1980s. The process was refined as a result of experience. Monitoring the process and learning the lessons of the experience was a particular priority of the two Mission Issues and Strategy Advisory Groups. Since 1973 there have been 65 PIM consultations of which the latest, for

West Africa, was held in Ghana in 1997. A staff member of the ACC was responsible for facilitating these consultations.

Provinces in the South have held the majority of consultations, inviting those churches and mission/development agencies with which they have had historical funding and personnel relationships. In some cases those who have held the purse strings have unduly influenced the agenda of their 'partners' who needed funds. The PIM process has also been influential in determining mission action and budget priorities for churches in the North. Despite problems, the PIM model of consultation over mission priorities has been a sustained attempt, over more than 20 years, to move from paternalism to partnership.

The programme has been of far-reaching significance as follows:

- It has helped churches focus on their mission calling and its priorities.
- It has provided a means of expression of mutual partnership that has extended far beyond the historic boards and agencies (but without neglecting them).
- It has enabled church representatives who perhaps did not have much contact with churches outside their own, to gain experience and carry it back to their home councils.
- It has provided a framework within which national church boards and voluntary agencies could focus their own priorities.
- It has helped get the language of partnership, of receiving and giving, of mutuality more into the bloodsteam of the Anglican Communion.
- It has encouraged widespread meeting.
- It has enabled a more effective sharing of resources of prayer, people and finances, and emphasized the importance of those non-tangible expressions of Christian experience.
- It resulted in the statement of 'Ten Principles of Partnership' produced by MISAG II in 1992.
- It established the principle of involving representatives of partners in assisting organizations, dioceses and provinces in planning for their future.

In recent years, the Partners-in-Mission process of consultations appears to have slowed to a virtual halt for a number of reasons:

- As provinces and dioceses have grown both in numbers and in size, so consultations have become more unwieldy and difficult (and costly) to organize.

- A generation of leaders has emerged who have not been part of the formative process.
- The growth in self-sufficiency and self-reliance in a number of provinces has lessened the urgency for them to seek financial support.
- The 1988 Lambeth Conference call for a Decade of Evangelism has been given greater attention, and more staff priority for the ACC.

The principles that underlie the PIM process, however, and the practical lessons learned must not be forgotten, but rather built upon and developed into the new context of the twenty-first century.

The 1990s

By the 1990s the Communion had become more complex and less amenable to centrally organized programmes, which, despite contrary intentions, were often dominated by Northern churches and their agencies. There are a number of factors in the changed situation.

There are now 38 provinces and over 618 dioceses. They are initiating a plethora of mission activities. In 1963 the major historic Northern national mission boards and missionary societies could be counted on the fingers of two hands. By the 1990s their resources in people and finance had decreased. Missionary personnel from the North have reduced in numbers. Apportionments from dioceses to the funds of national mission boards as well as individual gifts to mission agencies have reduced in real terms.

Alongside the historic organizations, new Northern agencies have emerged. They often focus on specific tasks such as team visits or development projects in specific countries. Although smaller than the older agencies, they often attract supporters because they seem new, participatory and personal.

Churches in the North, although struggling to renew themselves and respond to their own contexts, are smaller in numbers and financial strength, and face increased local demands. Churches in the South have increased in numbers and in some cases, in financial resources and are also aiming at self-reliance.

The significance of a whole range of links involving provinces, dioceses, cathedrals, parishes (individually and in groups) has increased.

The 1980s also saw the rapid growth of development agencies

in the North, emphasizing issues of development and justice. Some attracted government funding and increased giving from individuals, often in response to disasters. They were perceived to be providing rapid responses.

From many of the newer churches of the Communion, new forms of cross-cultural missionary engagement have emerged. There are now many new centres of missionary sending and receiving.

In 1899 an international mission map of the world would have resembled that of a steamship line with many of the routes traceable back to Britain, Europe and North America. In 1999 a cross-cultural mission map for the Anglican Communion and for other denominations now resembles a world airlines map with many centres and hubs, both internationally and within countries, and no overall centre. The possibilities of exchange, encounter, partnership, shared mission and evangelism are much greater, richer and less controllable. As the Communion grows, so the numbers of centres of mission sending will increase further.

Principles of Partnership

In 1993 the Anglican Consultative Council accepted the final report of the Second Mission Issues and Strategy Advisory Group (MISAG II). Its reflection on the PIM process identified 'Ten Principles of Partnership', which were proposed as 'essential to any meaningful or healthy partnership in mission process'. (The full text of these is included in appendix C.)

1	Local initiative	6	Integrity
2	Mutuality	7	Transparency
3	Responsible stewardship	8	Solidarity
4	Interdependence	9	Meeting together
5	Cross fertilization	10	Acting ecumenically

These principles stand as excellent 'benchmarks' against which to measure mission partnerships. They have been used creatively in some parts of the Communion and ignored in others.

Companion Diocese and Other Companionship Links

The system of diocesan companion links grew out of the call for MRI. Across the Communion they have to come to complement and add value to the historic connections through the national mission boards and missionary societies. At their best they expand awareness of the experiences of Christians in different parts of the Communion and encourage mutual support, challenge and learning. The face-to-face meeting they encourage is of great value in providing cohesion and flesh to the bones of the Communion's structures.

The number and variety of diocesan companion links has expanded considerably since the 1960s. Patterns of linking vary among provinces. For example, dioceses in the USA and Canada tend to link with one other diocese for a limited period. English diocesan companion links broaden this model to include those who link to a number of provinces. Many links also appear to have become permanent, with evaluation reviews seeking to improve the quality of the relationship. Whereas the guidelines suggest that transfer of money should not form a major feature of a companion link, in a number of instances financial support is large. There are increasing numbers of multilateral links such as the Dioceses of Bradford, Northern Sudan and Southwest Virginia, or Los Angeles, West Africa and Belize.

Given the expanding variety of diocesan links, it is important that the 'Companion Relationship Guidelines' and 'Principles of Partnership' be used to add value and quality to the links. The purpose of companion links is to assist the companions to get to know each other, to learn from each other and to each share their faith.

The mission and evangelism desk at the Anglican Communion Office maintains a list of formal links and a list of those dioceses seeking relationships. The selection of links is a haphazard process, which is perhaps inevitable within a Communion of autonomous provinces. Nevertheless efforts need to be made to enable those dioceses without links but seeking them, to find companions. The 1998 Lambeth Conference encouraged all dioceses to have some connection, formal or informal, by 2008, a process which needs to be facilitated and monitored by the mission and evangelism office.

Alongside the diocesan links there are an increasing number of other forms of companionship – between parishes, parish to diocese, between cathedrals, etc. A task for the next Mission

Commission is to assess this development and offer guidelines for new and more particular forms of companionship relationship. The existing 'Anglican Communion Companion Diocese Guidelines' could provide a basis.

Changing Expressions of Mission and Mission Connections

Various expressions of international and cross-cultural mission are emerging in many parts of the world. They are responses both to local contexts and to the missionary vocation. Some are a recovery and renewal of older forms. Others are new. Many of these new expressions of mission are reaching out to the least evangelized peoples and communities in our world, whether within nations or across geographical boundaries. The list below is not exhaustive, but is intended to increase awareness of what is happening within the Anglican Communion.

Forced movements of peoples

In recent years civil war, famine and other natural causes have tragically displaced a growing number of people, many of them Christian. Sadly this is not new in world history. Recent examples include Sudanese to Congo, Northern Uganda and Kenya; Mozambicans to Malawi; Rwandans to Tanzania, Uganda and Congo; displacement of populations within Liberia and Sierra Leone; Karen from Burma to Thailand. They worship in the midst of their suffering and share their faith with those around them. The accounts of their faithfulness and witness, and their success at forming new congregations are a challenge, rebuke and inspiration to other parts of the world church. It is a reminder that it was persecution that first caused the gospel to spread (Acts 8).

Natural movements of peoples

In recent decades, the movement of large numbers of people for reasons of business or emigration has led to the establishment of communities in countries other than their places of origin. The world is a much more pluralistic place as populations mix. As Christians have moved, so they have both joined the congregations of their new countries and also formed congregations in their own language and culture. In both ways they have often stimulated and contributed to the life and mission of the church within the country to which they have come. Again this natural movement is not new. It occurred in the first decade of the Church (Rom. 16).

Missionary chaplaincies

The movement of peoples has led to an increase of missionary chaplaincies set up to minister within the community and to assist the receiving church in its ministry among the community. Examples include the Nigerian chaplaincy in London; Korean chaplaincy in Toronto; over 30 such chaplaincies in Sydney; a Sabahan chaplain in W. Malaysia. The Diocese of New York has congregations in at least 12 different language groups.

Missionary bishops and formation of new dioceses

As a response to the call for a Decade of Evangelism, missionary bishops were named and missionary dioceses created in the largely Islamic northern Nigeria. They were financially sponsored by older dioceses in southern Nigeria, and in some cases by individuals. This has led to rapid church growth and yet further dioceses have been formed. In Kenya the formation of smaller geographical dioceses in some areas has enabled increased attention to be given to the growth of congregations. The 1998 Lambeth Conference identified this process as one for further study to see what lessons can be learned. This is an issue we refer to the next Mission Commission.

Missionary faith-sharing teams

There has been a growth in the sending of short-term, faith-sharing mission teams. Many examples can be given. They include South–North; South–South; North–South. They both increase the experience of the mainly lay Christians who participate, and enable missionary encounters to take place in the areas they visit. The diocesan bishop often leads diocesan teams. Renewal teams serve a similar function. Mission agencies like USPG and CMS have brought mission teams, drawn from a number of nations, to Britain. The Dioceses of Southwest Brazil and

Uruguay have used a team to establish a community on their joint border.

New missionary societies in the South

New missionary societies are being formed. The Church of Nigeria has formed the Church of Nigeria Missionary Society. This is a synodical society which is lay-led with money raised from voluntary contributions. To some extent it combines the model of ECUSA with that of CMS. In South India missionary societies have long been established and they are developing their work both within and outside India.

Multi-point (or multilateral) mission movements

There are a variety of patterns of joint mission partnerships between one or more Northern agencies and one or more Southern dioceses. The Church of Canada has supported Cuban missionaries to Uruguay; British SAMS and CMS, a Brazilian missionary to Mozambique; British CMS and USPG, a north Indian presbyter to Johannesburg for inter-faith ministry.

South–South mission

There is an increase in missionaries sent from one part of the South to another. The Diocese of Singapore sends both missionaries and mission teams to Latin America, South Africa, Thailand, Cambodia and Indonesia. Individual parishes provide the support, the sending diocesan bishop, on the recommendation of the Board of Mission, provides the authority and co-ordination. In Melanesia the Melanesian Brotherhood has sent missionaries to Papua New Guinea, Philippines and Fiji. Most Northern mission agencies now have budgets to assist South–South missionary encounter and exchange (a recommendation made by MISAG-II in 1992).

South–South Movement

The South–South Movement that arose from the Brisbane mission agencies conference in 1986 is one structure that has grown to encourage South–South connections. It is described in more detail below.

Networks

Within the Anglican Communion, networks have been developed which contribute to the mission, in its broad sense, of the Communion: justice and peace, youth, interfaith, refugees, etc. Networks provide flexible means of connection. They do not act as operational programmatic agencies in their own right, but they enable those who do to co-ordinate and consult. A network for mission and evangelism has been proposed as a result of the work of Section II of the 1998 Lambeth Conference. The process of networking is to be encouraged in a Communion as broad and diverse as ours.

Changes to the historic synodical mission boards and voluntary mission agencies

Historic mission agencies, both voluntary (like CMS and USPG) and synodical (like the Boards of ECUSA and the Anglican Church of Canada), have played a vital part in the growth of the Communion. During the 1990s, they too are responding to changes in the Communion and its context. Many have developed new mission statements, directions and priorities. In Canada, for example, the challenge is to connect international and domestic mission. In England a number of agencies are looking at ways to concentrate on mission partnership at the cutting edge of mission, and to work with churches in enabling them to respond to those priorities.

South to South Encounters

In 1994 in Nairobi and again in 1997 in Kuala Lumpur, representatives of Anglican churches in the South met to look at their mission. The conference aims are an important statement of their concerns:

- To meet, to know and to encourage one another in our faith and mission as Christians of the 'South'.
- To listen to God and to listen to one another.
- To share our stories, our needs, our resources, our vision.
- To explore and encourage ways of offering ourselves and our unique gifts and insights as Christians of the South for the enrichment of the life of the whole Church and for world mission.

- To discover our unique identity as Anglican Christians of the non-western world.
- To encourage qualitative and relevant leadership development for our rapidly growing churches so as to secure the future of the Church in the South and worldwide; to enable partnership, both South to South and South to North, on the basis of equality and mutual respect.
- To explore ways of being authentically Christian in our cultural milieu while remaining universally connected to the global Anglican Communion.

The South-to-South movement has named a steering committee and shows every sign of continuing with future gatherings.

One of the issues emerging from these conferences is the importance of capacity-building, by which is meant developing the skills and resources of churches and communities for greater self-reliance, self-confidence and self-direction.

Emerging Patterns of Contact and Co-ordination

Personnel exchange and encounter

In 1992, MISAG II emphasized the importance of encounter and exchange as a means of strengthening mission.

> Exchange necessarily involves the joyful sharing of resources [including] long and short-term personnel exchanged from south to south, south to north, north to south. Ideas, vision, respect for other peoples' culture and renewed energy and enthusiasm for mission can be the fruit of these exchanges. Visits will enhance an appreciation of liturgy, spirituality and tradition.[37]

Despite all the advances in technology, the value of person-to-person encounter and face-to-face meeting cannot be over-estimated.

Conferences

If PIM consultations have decreased, more general conferences are proving of increased importance in enabling contacts to be made, ideas to be shared and relationships to develop. The two South-to-South Encounters (Nairobi 1994; Kuala Lumpur 1997) have both established connections as well as making their own impact on the Communion. The 1995 Kanuga conference to mark the mid-point review of the Decade of Evangelism was an important gathering of laity, clergy and bishops from across the Communion. The 1998 Lambeth Conference provided opportunities for face-to-face meeting. These particular gatherings have also provided models of ways of meeting, and in particular, of the importance of worship, which have been carried into provincial and other gatherings.

Planning consultations

Some agencies and churches are holding consultations to assist them in their own priority setting. From Britain, USPG has held a number with individual partner churches and provinces, on its specific policies and programmes with its partner church. CMS has held three consultations (in Britain, Hong Kong and Uganda) on more general priorities for the future, drawing representatives from a wide range of partners. The Church of England 'Conference on the Church of England and its World Mission Partnership', held before the 1998 Lambeth Conference, was an important occasion for discerning issues to be addressed in the future. The Mothers' Union World-Wide Council, held before each Lambeth Conference, is a most significant occasion for women leaders of the Communion to meet. There are similar occasions in other parts of the Communion.

The value of these conferences can be greatly enhanced if conference participants visit local Christian communities to experience their life and outreach, and then take their experience back to their own areas. This also serves to encourage the host community.

International representatives

Other agencies, such as the Anglican Church of Canada, ensure that there are representatives of partner churches on their major boards, committees and councils. It is becoming increasingly common in the North for participants from the South to be included in gatherings as a matter of course.

Ecumenical structures

In many places there are increasing efforts at ecumenical co-ordination of mission activities. In the USA and Canada, for example, the orientation and debriefing of mission personnel is often undertaken jointly by several denominations pooling their resources. So, too, are resources for mission education frequently developed by an ecumenical working group.

Money and Mission Relationships

Experience has shown that money both benefits and distorts mission relationships. Because it is so significant we include a reflection on this issue.

Every dimension of mission requires money. The commonly used expressions, 'money makes the mill go round' or 'it takes cash to care' make it apparent that mission programmes must be adequately funded if they are to achieve the desired results. The records of the early Church show that from its inception, money was needed for mission and ministry, and those who had access to money made it available to the leaders. The account of Paul's collection from the poor churches of Greece and Asia Minor for the church in Jerusalem experiencing famine, is a model of the principles for sharing money (see 2 Cor. 8 and 9). The sharing of financial resources (often sacrificially, Phil. 4.10–17) was therefore an established principle within the body of Christ. It must also be noted, however, that the first major act of deception, the Ananias and Sapphira saga (Acts 5), was centred on money, bringing into focus the fact that there is not only a bright side to money, but a dark side also.

Those who engage with others as partners in mission, must commit themselves to the biblical principles of Christian stewardship and ensure that money transfers are made on the basis of transparency, responsibility and accountability. Transparency refers to the source of the funds, the purpose of giving and the legitimacy of the project. Responsibility requires that those on the receiving end must demonstrate their commitment by making their own contribution to the project. Accountability is the means of ensuring that the money is used in the most efficient manner for the purpose for which it is needed and intended. With the appropriate safeguards, the giving and receiving of money can indeed be a blessing to both giver and receiver, though one may argue on the basis of Scripture that the greater blessing goes to the giver.

Money, however, has its darker side. Money can be given to maintain power, control and influence. 'The one who pays the piper calls the tune' is an old saying that cannot be ignored. Integrity demands that those who are receivers must reject all funds where the source and intention are either unclear or unacceptable. This applies not only in church-to-church exchanges, but also in government to church or business to church.

Another reality about the dark side of money is that it may engender greed. 'The love of money is a root of all kinds of evil' (1 Tim. 6.10). Those who control its disbursement may 'feather their own nests' instead of fostering development. There is no need to give examples of the misuse of funds caused by greed. It is a common human failing from which many church leaders have not been exempt. Appropriate mechanisms and checks for accounting must be employed to keep those who receive and spend money away from the snare of this temptation.

Another negative feature of the sharing of money is the propensity to foster dependence on the outside donor. Much has been written about the danger of creating a 'dependency syndrome' in 'receiving churches'. The 'Three Self Principles', enunciated by Henry Venn of CMS in the nineteenth century, have been promoted as a way of charting a course that would see new churches taking responsibility for the various areas of their life in terms of governance, support and propagation. Money unwisely given and received can have the effect of creating dependence, rather than building capacity.

Finally, money can have a negative effect on the donor. It can focus the donor's concern on the raising of funds, on its transfer and on seeking to control its use, thus taking attention away from other more significant aspects of partnership.

None of the foregoing cautions, however, can override the basic principle that sharing, which includes the sharing of money, must continue to be an integral part of what is meant by partnership in mission. A holistic approach sees financial sharing as a dimension of total partnership which includes the sharing of joys, sorrows, people, liturgies, prayer, challenge, advocacy, experience of poverty for the sake of the kingdom.

Structures for Co-ordination: Within Provinces

On the principle that mission movements and provincial structures are both expressions of Christian discipleship, there need to be, within provinces, means to ensure that there is adequate communication and sharing of plans and activities. Different churches will develop different models. What is important is that there is opportunity for connecting and sharing. Some examples of current structures follow:

- In the USA, the Episcopal Council for Global Mission was formed in 1990 as a forum in which representatives of a wide range of dioceses, large congregations, mission agencies, religious orders and the national church boards, including the relief board, can all meet. This has proved highly effective in building relations and developing mutual understanding. The structure is simple, workable and acceptable to all. In 2000 this became the Episcopal Church's official Partnership for Global Mission (EPGM).
- In England, the Partnership for World Mission (PWM) was formed in 1978 to provide a forum in which representatives of the mission agencies and General Synod could meet and work together. In 1991 it became a constituent part of the General Synod Board of Mission, in an endeavour to allow international mission and mission in England to inform each other.
- In Melanesia, the Melanesian Board of Mission includes the Melanesian Brotherhood and Sisterhood, the Community of the Sisters of the Church, the Mothers' Union, the Missions to Seamen. It is also responsible for youth ministry, hospital and prison chaplaincies, and evangelism.
- In Australia, mission agencies, including the synodical Anglican Board of Mission and voluntary mission agencies, like CMS and SAMS, have formed a mission agency network.
- The Church in Wales has a Partnership for World Mission Committee consisting of representatives of mission agencies and chaired by a nominee of the House of Bishops.

Structures of Co-ordination: For the Anglican Communion

An Inter-Anglican Standing Commission on Mission

Although mission is carried on within each province, the underlying principle of the Communion that each church needs the wider Church to assist, critique and provide stimulation, argues for some real but light international co-ordination of mission and evangelism across provinces and mission agencies. In the past this has been provided first by the Mission Issues and Strategy Advisory Groups – MISAG I (1980–5) and MISAG II (1986–92), followed by a Standing Commission on Mission, known as MISSIO (1994–9) established by ACC-9 in Cape Town, 1993.

The expanding diversity of mission connections within the Communion, the priority given to mission and evangelism by the Decade of Evangelism, and the 1988 and 1998 Lambeth Conferences, all point to the continuation of the current Standing Commission on Mission for the Anglican Communion. Its basic purpose should be to enable the sharing of information and reflection, and the facilitation of relationships across provinces and synodical and voluntary mission agencies. Its membership should include representatives both of synodical and voluntary mission agencies, and of the wider Church.

It is proposed that the title MISSIO be replaced by the title Inter-Anglican Standing Commission on Mission. Details of the proposal, including suggested membership and ways of working, are included as a separate section at the end of the chapter.

A mission staff officer at the Anglican Communion Office

The functions of a Mission Commission and the growing rich variety and complexity of mission activities and relationships in the Communion support the reinstatement of a senior-level staff person in the mission and evangelism office, with appropriate secretarial support. Such a post is as important for the future as for the past. The international mission relationships and connections of the Communion are significant means of providing cohesion, coherence and human experience that flesh out the realities of worldwide Anglicanism. Details of the major functions of the staff position are included with the proposal for the Standing Commission on Mission at the end of the chapter.

A number of the networks of the Communion are engaged in mission in its broad understanding. So it would be appropriate for the Mission and Evangelism Officer to be the point of contact between them and the Anglican Communion Office. This would enable the officer to keep the Mission Commission and the networks abreast of what each is doing.

Partnership to Companionship?

There has been a significant narrowing of the meaning of the term 'partnership' in the 1990s. The word is increasingly used to describe specific programmes or collaborative activity between agencies or dioceses, so that there is talk of mission partnerships. This is a change from earlier broader usage of 'partnership' to describe the total relationship that should exist between churches. Drawn from the word *koinonia*, it has its roots in that relationship of sharing found within the life of the Trinity, into which Christians are drawn through Christ, and into which God's mission is to draw the whole inhabited world (Eph. 1.9, 10; Col. 1.15–20).

That quality of broad relationship may now better be described by the word 'companionship'. The word speaks of those who are equals taking part in a journey together, relating, supporting, encouraging, communicating, breaking bread and being together. There cannot be a dominant companion, for if there is, the companionship breaks up. It also carries the connotation of solidarity: standing with each other in times of struggle and suffering.

Companionship speaks of values, trust, listening, generosity, encouragement, support and sharing; of journeying together in the movement of the Church. It provides a different and creative context in which to speak of programmes and budgets. It is that quality of relationship among Christians that will encourage real witness of life and word, and enable Christians to push beyond what now exists. In a Church of England consultation about good and bad experiences of mission partnership, good partnership experiences had to do with relationships, attitudes and values – respect, generosity, openness, care, listening, mutuality, prayer, worship, encouragement, support in situations of injustice, sharing in struggles, good personal relationships enabling free and frank exchange. In bad experiences some or all of these were lacking.

It has taken several decades for the term 'partnership' to become part of the currency of the Communion. It should not be lost, but it may now be time to build on it and speak more the language of companions in order to encourage this breadth and depth of quality in mission relationships.

International and Local Mission

One of the challenges facing the Communion is how to enable the international experience of mission to inform and have an impact on the local experience – sometimes called inner, domestic or home mission. Various structures have been tried. But it may be that the clue is to be found within the concept of a companionship in which the journey of churches together sees matters of money, people and programmes as instruments to ensure mutual sharing at the deeper level of experience, struggle, prayer, engagement with context in order to be transformed and so transform.

An example of what this might involve is found in the recent experience of the Anglican Church of Canada. That experience is much wider than an issue of partnership and so it is included as a separate chapter, but among its themes is the struggle to relate international partnership practice to local Canadian concerns.

Questions for Reflection and Discussion

- What lessons and principles does your province, diocese, mission agency draw from the Partners in Mission process? In what ways can they be improved to assist your work?
- What are the structures for consultation and co-ordination between voluntary agencies and the wider Church in your parish, diocese and province? How do you evaluate their effectiveness? How can they be improved?
- What new expressions of mission do you see developing in your parish, diocese, province and the wider Anglican Communion? How does your church/agency connect with them? What does it learn from them? What ecumenical mission activities/structures are found in your region?
- How are representatives of other parts of the Anglican Communion and wider Church involved in your committees, councils, decision-making

and consultative processes? How adequate is this? How might it be improved?

- In what ways does the budget of your agency, diocese, province contribute to South–South mission?
- What have been your experiences over the use of money for mission? How have you been able to use it to positive effect? How have you been able to overcome the problems of allowing it to distort transparent, mutual and open mission relationships?
- How have you used the Ten Principles of Partnership within your agency, diocese, province? How could you use them more effectively?
- What do you think of using the language of companionship to give new meaning to partnership in mission?
- The Lambeth Conference called for all dioceses to have some form of formal or informal companionship link by 2008 – what new forms of connection for mission with other dioceses can you imagine?

Recommendations

In response to the Lambeth Conference Resolution 2:2e on 'Mission and the Structures of the Anglican Communion', and having heard of the proposed recommendations of the ACC Joint Standing Committee's Priorities Working Group, MISSIO:

- Endorses the proposal of the Priorities Working Group to continue a Standing Commission on Mission.
- Recommends that it be called the Inter-Anglican Standing Commission on Mission, with functions and membership as detailed below.
- Recommends that a senior-level mission and evangelism staff officer be appointed to the Anglican Communion Office, responsible for the functions listed below.

Inter-Anglican Standing Commission on Mission

The Commission on Mission shall be appointed by and accountable to the Anglican Consultative Council or its standing committee.

Tasks and functions of the Commission

1 Be accountable to ACC.

- To report and receive tasks from the Anglican Consultative Council.

2 Oversee mission relationships.

- To facilitate companion diocese and other companionship links throughout the Communion, in accordance with the guidelines for such links.

- To work with Anglican networks for mission and evangelism as they currently exist or might emerge in the future.
- To facilitate the sharing of resources, both human and financial, throughout the Communion.
- To link, share and critique experiences of capacity-building for mission and evangelism.

3 Reflection.

- To engage in theological reflection on mission. This would include but not be limited to, reflections on gospel and culture, on the Missio Dei, on the transformation of the Church, on the implications of the changing profile of the Anglican Communion, on the good news in situations of poverty, displacement, war and conflict.
- To be a forum where the provinces and the voluntary and synodical mission agencies of the Communion share and reflect on their practices, experiences and learnings of mission and evangelism.

4 Priority of mission and evangelism.

- To continue the momentum of the Decade of Evangelism, in accordance with the learnings described elsewhere in this report. This includes encouraging the Anglican Communion to see mission and evangelism as a gospel imperative, not an optional activity.

5 New structures.

- To encourage the emergence of new and appropriate structures for mission and evangelism.
- To liaise with the South-to-South Movement.

6 Ecumenical expressions

- To encourage, monitor and learn from ecumenical expressions of mission.

Membership of the Commission

Membership of the Commission shall be appointed by the ACC standing committee with intention to include a mix of the following factors:

- Expertise in missiology.
- Gender balance.
- Balance of clergy/lay.
- Voluntary mission agencies and synodical mission boards from both North and South. Seven members from this category with at least three from the South.

- Knowledge of or involvement with province/region/Anglican Communion.
- Continuity with MISSIO of up to six continuing members.
- Eighteen appointed from nominations submitted by the provinces of the Communion:

Region	Provinces	Number
North American and Caribbean	USA, Canada, CPWI	2
Latin America	Cono Sur, Brazil, Central America, Caribe	2 (1 Spanish speaker, 1 Portuguese speaker)
Europe	England, Scotland, Wales, Ireland	2
East Africa	Kenya, Tanzania, Sudan, Uganda, Rwanda, Burundi, Congo, Indian Ocean	2 (1 francophone, 1 anglophone)
West Africa	Nigeria, West Africa	1
Southern/Central Africa	CPSA, Central Africa	2
Middle East and sub-continent	Jerusalem and Middle East, Ceylon, CSI, CNI, Pakistan, Bangladesh	2
Australasia	Australia, Aotearoa, New Zealand and Polynesia, Melanesia, PNG	3
East Asia	Philippines, Japan, Korea, South East Asia, Hong Kong, Myanmar (Burma)	2

- Members-at-large, these to be appointed to balance the six factors listed above.

- The chairperson to be appointed by the ACC, either from among the provincial members or as a member-at-large.
- A liaison member from ACC.
- There shall be rotating membership, term by term within a region, to ensure variation in membership.

Modus operandi of the Commission

- The Commission shall meet four times during its five-year term of office, with meetings lasting for approximately ten days plus travel time.
- Members are expected to undertake tasks between meetings.
- It is recommended that the chairperson appoint an advisory group of two or three members who can function as a decision-making executive between meetings.

Mission Staff Person at the Anglican Communion Office

It is recommended that the staff vacancy in the mission and evangelism office be filled as soon as possible, with the following functions to be included in the job description:

- To ensure that the Inter-Anglican Standing Commission on Mission receives the staff support needed to accomplish its work.
- To offer leadership and suggest new initiatives for the work of mission and evangelism in the Anglican Communion, as appropriate.
- To be the mission liaison/connector with the appropriate Anglican Communion networks and with the South-to-South Movement.
- To liaise with provincial mission officers/secretaries.
- To liaise with synodical mission boards and voluntary mission agencies.
- To ensure good communication and the sharing of information around the Communion re mission and evangelism experiences/stories/resources.
- To oversee the development of various kinds of companion links within the Communion.

7

The Struggle for Transformation

Journey of Repentance: The Anglican Church of Canada's Struggle for Transformation

This is a story about the 'dark side' of the missionary endeavour, of the consequences of cultural arrogance, of how succeeding generations are struggling to address the 'sins of the parents'. This is a story of the Anglican Church of Canada's journey of repentance.

In Canada during the colonial period (pre-1867) and well into the twentieth century, colonizers from Europe moved across the country from east to west, seizing land, settling farmsteads, bringing their own notions of government, law and order, as well as their own interpretation of Christianity. The original inhabitants, or First Nations of the land were killed, displaced, converted. Newcomers and original inhabitants did not understand one another, but it soon became clear to the indigenous people that the newcomers were stronger and they intended to stay permanently. As in other parts of the colonized world, these newcomers from Europe believed their culture to be superior, progressive and 'civilized', while the ways of the indigenous inhabitants were termed pre-civilized at best, or more often barbaric and savage.

Throughout most of the nineteenth century and the first half of the twentieth century, the articulated goal of the federal government of Canada, the churches, most non-indigenous Canadians, and even some indigenous First Nations was that of assimilation. The belief was that the way forward for indigenous people was to learn the languages and cultures of the colonizers (French and English), to be trained for jobs and gradually to be absorbed, with their own indigenous ways of life disappearing over time. The main vehicle for implementing this policy of assimilation was residential schools. It was thought that the quickest route to 'civilizing' and 'converting' the indigenous population was to remove indigenous children from their homes and communities, to place them in residential schools, to forbid them to speak their mother tongue, to condemn their cultures as barbaric and their spirituality as heathen. The early missionaries had a strong commitment to basic education which they believed was essential to the survival and advancement of indigenous children. So with the best of intentions towards the indigenous people, they started the first schools. By the end of the nineteenth century, a partnership had developed between the government and the churches, with the government providing the bulk of the funds and the churches operating the schools on behalf of the government. In the case of the Anglican Church, the schools were run by the Missionary Society of the Church in Canada (MSCC).

Between 1820 and 1969, the Anglican Church of Canada administered 26 Indian residential schools, the Roman Catholics administered over 60 schools and other churches approximately 15.

By the 1960s in Canada, there was growing unease in all the churches about the residential schools, both their practices, and the basic philosophy underlying their existence. The Anglican Church commissioned Charles Hendry to undertake a major study of the relationships between the church and aboriginal peoples, and his report, *Beyond Traplines*, received by the General Synod of 1969, resulted in a significant shift in church policy. At that time the church withdrew from the residential schools project and committed itself to trying to build a new, improved and more just relationship with its indigenous members, as well as advocating on behalf of the indigenous population at large.

During the 1970s and 1980s, the Anglican Church worked slowly but surely to improve the position of its indigenous members through hiring a Co-ordinator for Native Ministries in the national office, and putting in place a national Council for Native Ministries to oversee and give direction to the work. In its justice work, the church began to advocate on behalf of indigenous peoples, and supported their struggles with the government for settlement of their many land claims. When the federal government established a Royal Commission on Aboriginal Peoples, the Anglican Church prepared and presented a brief outlining its own participation in the government policy of assimilation, through its partnership with the government in the residential schools system.

In 1993, at the Second Native Convocation of Indigenous Anglicans which took place at Minaki Lodge in Ontario, Archbishop Michael Peers issued an apology on behalf of the whole Church for the harm done by the residential schools system. Here is an excerpt from that apology:

> I accept and I confess before God and you, our failures in the residential schools. We failed you. We failed ourselves. We failed God. I am sorry, more than I can say, that we were part of a system which took you and your children from home and family. I am sorry, more than I can say, that we tried to remake you in our image, taking from you your language and the signs of your identity. I am sorry, more than I can say, that in our schools so many were abused physically, sexually, culturally and emotionally. On behalf of the Anglican Church of Canada, I offer our apology.

This apology is a public acknowledgement of the sin of racism and ethnic superiority. This sin was and is perpetuated against indigenous people in Canada. It is a sin also against the Creator in whose image we are all made. The missionary movement in general has frequently, though not always, been guilty of this sin. But racism/ethnic superiority is also one of the underlying causes of the failure of many of our current attempts throughout the Anglican Communion to establish partnership relationships based on respect, mutual responsibility and interdependence. While this apology has been graciously accepted by indigenous Anglicans, there are many indigenous people who have left the Church in anger and are either unaware of this apology, or have rejected it.

The current plight of indigenous people in Canadian society at the end of this twentieth century is a national disgrace. The rates of crime, family violence, alcohol and drug abuse, unemployment and incarceration are way above the national average. Many communities and families are dysfunctional, their people in despair and crying out for help. While the roots of today's problems may be the historical policy of assimilation implemented through the residential schools systems, the crisis is very much a present crisis of today. The churches and the government have been too slow to respond, and in their frustration, many indigenous people are choosing litigation in their search for justice and reparation. This is proving to be a very painful process for all parties, both plaintiffs and defendants, and does not lead to reconciliation. It is also proving to be very expensive. All parties are now aware that alternatives to litigation are needed. Alternative approaches include 'truth-telling' and 'truth-receiving', formal and personalized apologies, compensaton/reparation, and memorialization of people's experiences. These approaches are difficult but necessary steps in beginning to make amends for a shameful past. The churches, in obedience to the gospel, are particularly concerned to work towards healing and reconciliation. The Anglican Church, for its part, established a Healing and Reconciliation Fund in 1993 and has increased the staffing to work at this long-term task. The government has recently followed suit with its own Aboriginal Healing Foundation. It remains to be seen whether these measures will be successful.

In 1994, during the Anglican Church of Canada's Fourth PIM Consultation, a group of indigenous Anglicans articulated their vision of a new covenant relationship between indigenous and non-indigenous members of the church. Here is an excerpt from the covenant statement:

> We acknowledge that God is calling us to a prayerful dialogue towards self-determination for us, the Indigenous People, within the Anglican Communion in Canada. Through this new relationship we can better respond to the challenges facing us in a relevant and meaningful way.
>
> As faithful people of God, guided by the Holy Spirit, we invite you, the Anglican Communion of Canada to covenant with us, the Indigenous Anglicans of Canada, in our vision of a new and enriched journey.
>
> Under the guidance of God's Spirit we agree to do all we can to call our people into unity in a new, self-determining community within the Anglican Church of Canada. To this end, we extend the hand of partnership to all those who will help us build a truly Anglican Indigenous Church in Canada. May God bless this new vision and give us grace to accomplish it. Amen.

This vision is of unity, community and self-determination, to be achieved within the Church not through separation. Given not only the historical record, but also the on-going plight of indigenous people in Canadian society, it is astonishing that, by the grace of God, there are still indigenous people who want to remain in the Church, and further, that they are graciously offering a hand of partnership to the rest of the Church so that all may journey together to healing and wholeness. The realization of this vision will require changes to existing structures and practices. While the covenant has been affirmed by the whole Church at the General Synod level, there continues to be lack of understanding and acceptance in some dioceses and parishes where change needs to happen. The question remains as to whether the dominant non-indigenous church can relinquish power and control while continuing to walk in partnership, offering financial support and being open to learn from the indigenous minority church.

This case study in cross-cultural mission is a sobering one. The sin of racism/ethnic superiority, coupled with the confusion of gospel and culture, has had devastating effects on the many and varied First Nations in Canada. 'The sins of the parents are visited on their children to the third and fourth generation', and the Anglican Church of Canada is currently reaping the fruits of those sins. Mission is indeed about proclaiming the good news of God's love through Jesus Christ, but it is also about affirming that all of humankind is created in God's image, with no group having the right to recreate others according to its own limited vision. So where the missionary project has a shameful and arrogant history, mission today must be about humility, repentance, justice and reparation. In the Anglican Church of Canada, we are on a journey towards reconciliation. It is going to be a long and difficult journey, but with God's grace, we will journey in partnership, indigenous and non-indigenous Anglicans together, and as a Church, as the people of God, we may eventually achieve reconciliation and be transformed in the process.

Reflections from a South African Perspective

The South African story can offer some helpful suggestions to the Canadian situation. In post-apartheid South Africa, the government set up a Truth and Reconciliation Commission as a means of bringing to light the truth and enabling people to put their stories behind them and move forward into a brighter future. The key elements in this process were the telling of individual stories, the listening to and honouring of those experiences, the acknowledgement of wrongdoing and apology, and finally, the acceptance of apology and a willingness to move forward.

While the process is by no means finished, nonetheless it is clear that it has been very helpful to very many people to have had opportunity to tell their stories and to have had those stories heard and recorded. The importance of public apology cannot be overstated. The question of reparation is not easily resolved, especially where the government's resources are limited. Also, it is not clear what the next steps will be in cases where amnesty has not been granted.

The Anglican Church of Canada might be helped in its journey towards reconciliation by inviting partners, including those from the Church of the Province of Southern Africa, to share their own experiences and learnings. It may also wish to share this painful journey with other parts of the Communion so that as we go forward in mission we may avoid repeating the errors of the past.

Reflections from a Zimbabwean Perspective

Land dispossession in post-colonial countries in the Anglican Communion remains a sensitive and volatile issue affecting the Church and its mission. It is a justice issue of major proportions.

The war of liberation in Zimbabwe was mainly about land dispossession affecting the black majority of the country. The Church (missionary church) was an accomplice in the process of dispossession. Cecil Rhodes, who occupied the country (which was later named after him – Rhodesia), found it convenient to dispossess Africans, and gave tracts of land to missionaries in order that they could establish mission stations. Forceful eviction of Africans was used to create room for mission farms. Unlike the Church in the Province of Southern Africa, the Church in Zimbabwe has remained silent on the issue and thus failed to fulfil its Christian responsibility to thousands of rural peasants who are barely surviving on arid land. Most of the mission farms are surrounded by landless rural folk. The situation has been made worse by new land dispossessors in the persons of black elite who have now joined settler farmers in denying the majority of the Africans access to land for their livelihood. The Church has a mission to preach justice if it is to be credible (Amos 3.5, Luke 4).

Reflections from an Australian Perspective

The dispossession of Aboriginal and islander peoples of their traditional lands, coupled with the policy of assimilation involving the removal of children from their families, has resulted in a desparate need for a process of reconciliation. One issue has become a powerful and emotional one in the reconciliation debate. It is the issue of an apology.

At the 1997 National Reconciliation Convention, Prime Minister John Howard offered indigenous Australians a personal but not a national apology for the wrongs done to them. The nearly 2,000 delegates responded with this resolution.

> We note that leaders across the social spectrum expressed their own personal apologies and sorrow for the treatment of indigenous peoples; this was itself an historic moment. We call on all parliaments, local governments, organizations and institutions to follow this lead with their own form of apology so that we can all move forward together to share responsibility for the future of this nation.

Since then, at the grass roots, many initiatives have been taken including 'sorry books' in which millions of white Australians have recorded their apologies. The churches, not least the Anglican Church in Australia, have provided materials and leadership for rational discussion and debate. The Church is supporting Governor General Sir William Deane who said: 'The past is never fully gone. It is absorbed into the present and the future. It stays to shape what we are and what we do.' Australians need reminding that they may be individually blameless for past wrongs, but must share responsibility for their outcome in present injustice. The fourth of the Five Marks of Mission (ACC, 1984 and 1990) needs emphasis in Australia as in Canada.

Questions for Reflection and Discussion

- Has the church in your province (diocese, parish) any historical sins of which it needs to repent? If so, how is it addressing this legacy?

- This case study states that repentance, apology, justice and reparation must precede reconciliation. Do you think each of these steps is necessary, and if so, why?

8

Prayers for the Mission of the Church

These prayers were gathered from around the Communion during the Decade of Evangelism. At the end of each prayer the source and diocese, province or individual who contributed the prayer is acknowledged.

Being Sent

Send out your Spirit in all creation
and fill the world with your glory.
Fire us with your power
Light us with your Word
And feed us with your living bread.
(Sheffield Diocese, England)

O God our Father, as you sent your Son, send us into this your world with your compelling love. Help us by your Spirit, to share your Gospel of love and forgiveness, of justice and peace, of compassion and care. Revive your Church and save your people. Through Jesus Christ our Lord. Amen.
(Diocese of Southwell, England)

Commitment

(*Response: 'Renew us in your love'*)
Pour out your Spirit on this land that we may know the things
    belonging to your peace.
Lord, in your mercy hear our prayer
Pour out your Spirit upon the Church that we may be found
    faithful in witness.
Lord, in your mercy hear our prayer
Pour out your Spirit upon our diocese that we may be united in the
    work to which you have called us.
Lord in your mercy hear our prayer
(*Church of Ireland Book of Occasional Prayer*,
Diocese of Cork, Cloyne and Ross, Ireland)

Pour out your Spirit upon our parish that our fellowship may be
   built up in love.
Lord, in your mercy hear our prayer
Pour out your Spirit upon our families that Christ may dwell with
   us.
Lord, in your mercy hear our prayer
Pour out your Spirit upon me that I may live in Christ.
Lord, in your mercy hear our prayer
(Armagh 21 Century Forward Together,
Diocese of Armagh, Ireland)

Empowerment

God of mountain, river and plain, of scattered centres and rural
   town,
of people black and white,
Inspire us by your Spirit with the message of your good news,
And fill us with desire to share your love with all.
Through Jesus Christ our Lord. Amen.
(Diocese of Bathurst, Australia)

God our heavenly Father, you revealed to us your only son, Jesus
Christ who became the reconciler of your people to you through
his awful death on the cross. He chose disciples to continue teaching and revealing him as Lord and Saviour. We ask you to open
our hearts and let Christ live in us that we would be his present
and future disciples for his mission. We pray that the radiant rays
of the Holy Spirit may inspire, and strengthen us to preach Christ
Jesus as Lord, Saviour and Life-Giver throughout the world. In
Jesus' name we pray. Amen.
(Diocese of Central Zambia, Central Africa)

Labourers

Almighty God, whose will it is that all should be saved and come to
the knowledge of the truth; send forth labourers into the harvest,
that all may know you, the one true God, and Jesus Christ whom
you sent, our only Lord and Saviour. Amen.
(NZ Board of Mission, New Zealand)

Almighty and everlasting God, who desires that all may be saved, the harvest is plentiful but labourers are few. Send more labourers into the field. Men and women, who will yield unconditionally to your divine service. And as your son, our Lord, said, if he be lifted up from the earth, he would draw all people unto him.

Grant that these labourers shall be vessels unto honour in your hands, through whom love will reach to those who know you not, and that soon the knowledge of you will cover the earth as the waters cover the sea and the kingdoms of the world become your kingdom, through Jesus Christ our Lord. Amen.
(Diocese of Jalingo, Nigeria)

Leaders

Loving and Eternal God, you never fail us. Touch your Church with your loving kindness. May your bishops who bear the vision of your Church lead us in fulfilling your will. May the clergy minister as faithful pastors the flock committed to their care, and may the people of God be continually renewed by the power of the Holy Spirit so as to give praise and glory to you. Through Jesus Christ our Lord. Amen.
(The Revd Canon Roger Chung,
Decade of Evangelism Co-ordinator,
Province of the Indian Ocean)

Almighty God and heavenly Father, we praise and glorify your holy name for your constant love and wisdom. We pray for all evangelism co-ordinators, teams and all resource persons around the world. May you open your blessing and wisdom to strengthen your dear sons and daughters who have dedicated their time and life to promote and expand your message of salvation. Protect and guide your servants and may your name be praised. We do submit before you our evangelism strategies for the next millennium that you should bless them and make them a success. In the Lord's name we pray. Amen.
(The Episcopal Church of the Sudan)

We pray, O Lord, for the bishops and clergy and lay pastors. Empower them with your calling to exercise faithful ministry of evangelism. Give them, O Lord, a fruitful harvest, especially in the establishment of new congregations and the strengthening of

existing ones. May they do all things to the honour and glory of
your son, Jesus Christ. Amen,
(Diocese of Honduras, Central America)

Millennium

Good Lord, we pray for the generation in the third millennium, so
that through them you would build a strong and spiritual Church.
Amen.
(Diocese of Buye, Burundi)

Personal

This is my whole life, O Lord:
to know your word and teach it;
to know your word and live it.
Teach me, O Lord, to proclaim what you teach
and to live how you live; through Jesus Christ. Amen.
(Diocese of Jos, Nigeria)

Lord God
Renew your Church
and begin with me,
Heal our land
tend our wounds
And make us one,
And use us in your service;
For Jesus Christ's sake
Lord of the Church
Make us the Church of the Lord. Amen.
(Diocese of Natal, Southern Africa)

Heavenly light, look on me
Give your blessing oh I cry
Confused and troubled in this world
Look upon me save my soul.
Thou art the noble son who dispels misery
The Hero of Golgotha who saved this world
The Bountiful 'Gupera' with blessings most
The most precious gift to a sinner like me
Thou art the Good News needed most

The eternal life that renews every soul
The God of God who shows the way of salvation
The wisest Counsel who sought to help a fool like me.
(Tamil, Sri Lanka)

Father in heaven, as I walked along the streets, help me to pray for
the people I meet who seem to be worn or worried. Save me from
grumbling about the state of this country. I ask for the help of the
Holy Spirit in being your witness and presence in your world
today. Amen.
(The Rt Revd John Sentamu
Diocese of Stepney, London, UK)

Repentance

We confess that we have been so busy with mending nets
that we have forgotten to go to fish.
Make us today fishermen
so that even if we come back home without fish we will be happy
because we have fed a lot of them. For Christ's sake. Amen.
(Diocese of South Western Brazil)

Almighty God, the Father of our Saviour Jesus Christ, you lowered
and humbled yourself for our sake, you also invited us to 'come and
let us reason together with you'. May we be reminded of your un-
selfish love in that you loved us and gave your son Jesus Christ.
Help us to be ready to forgive and forget just as you always
forgive and forget our sins. Through Jesus Christ our Lord. Amen.
(Anglican Church of Kenya)

Too often we are without love, ungracious, foolish and wondering
in darkness. We live in our own confusion and it is a cold fearsome
place. Lift our eyes to your son, the Christ of Calvary, in all his
stark loneliness that we might know the sweetness of being for-
given, the fragrance of being accepted, the power of being set free
for service, the joy of being strengthened in faith. In the warm
fellowship of your people awakened by the Holy Spirit, refresh us
and renew us, challenge us and change us that, resting in the warm
cradle of our Father's love, we may be channels of the love, grace,
wisdom and light of the Lord Jesus, that his kingdom may be

displayed and his Church re-created through him who served in humility and reigns in glory ever Jesus Christ our Lord. Amen.
(Newhills Parish Church, Aberdeen, Scotland)

Spiritual Warfare

The battle belongs to the Lord
Lord Jesus, the Captain of the army, enable us to recognize your leadership as we fight to set people free from the power of evil. Under your leadership we will win. Help us never to depend on our own energy and resources only. Give us fresh vision of your love as we march on to conquer new territories for you. Amen.
(Bishop Henry Orombi
Diocese of Nebbi, Uganda)

Vision

O God our heavenly Father,
you are the author and source of the great commandment and the
    great commission.
Grant us vision for evangelism now and into the next millennium.
We pray for the poor, the maimed and displaced, we pray for
    theological students from our institutions, may they be aware
    of the commandment and commission.
Make us to be light and salt of the earth.
Within all the pomp and pageantry of our tradition, make the
    people to see that humble man from Galilee,
in whose name we ask. Amen.
(Province of Myanmar)

Vision and direction from on high
Father God, whose desire is for every nation, tribe, people and language to be saved. Lord we who are your chosen ones, seek direction for the salvation of the people of our land and beyond, for without knowledge your people perish. Amen.
(Diocese of West Malaysia, South East Asia)

Father, pour out your Spirit upon your people,
and grant us:
a new vision for your glory
a new faithfulness to your word,

a new consecration to your service,
that your love may grow among us, and your kingdom come.
Through Jesus Christ our Lord. Amen.
(Diocese of Bunbury, Australia)

Witness

Almighty God, by your grace you have given us new life in Jesus
Christ. By your Spirit you have called us to proclaim his name
throughout the world. Awaken in us such a love for you and your
work, that in the Decade of Evangelism we may so boldly proclaim
Jesus Christ in word and deed, that all people may come to know
him as Saviour and follow him as Lord, to the glory of your name.
Amen.
(Anglican Fellowship of Prayer
Diocese of Central Newfoundland, Canada)

Almighty God, we praise you for the joy of belonging to you, and
for the joy of knowing that you love all people with the same everlasting love. You have made us so different from each other, and
yet in Jesus Christ we are one community of diverse races, cultures
and languages. As you have sent your son into the world to do your
will, so give us the courage and the strength to accept his call to be
his witnesses, and to do his will that your Church here on earth
may fulfil the purpose of your salvation; through the same Jesus
Christ our Lord, who lives and reigns with you, and the Holy
Spirit, ever one God, now and ever. Amen.
(Diocese of North East India, CNI)

May we follow your commandment
To become witness of the Lord to the end of the earth
Let us proclaim the gospel to the poor, the blind,
The prisoners, and the least elsewhere
Inspired by the faith of the evangelists who followed Jesus Christ
So that we may open 40 new churches
Through which we may dedicate our prayer,
Sacrifice and life for your love.
(The Anglican Church of Korea)

Almighty God, make us faithful witnesses in the mission of your
Church during this Decade of Evangelism. Help us to seek justice,

work for healing and salvation of our nations (Vanuatu and Solomon Islands). Renew and empower us with your Holy Spirit for the establishment of your kingdom in these islands so diverse in tongue and race through Jesus Christ our Lord. Amen.
(The Church of the Province of Melanesia)

9

Resources for Mission and Evangelism: Training and Tools

A list of some of the resources used and recommended by provinces and dioceses of the Communion during the Decade of Evangelism. A complete list is available from Mission and Evangelism Department, Anglican Communion Office, Partnership House, 157 Waterloo Road, London SE1 8UT, UK. Each entry lists the province/diocese which made the recommendation.

Preparation and Training

Envisioning/planning

Action Plans, Rebecca McClain and James Magers.
How to make effective action plans.
Available from: Parish Services, 1201 Chestnut St, Suite 1200, Philadelphia, PA 19107, USA.
Province/diocese: ECUSA.

Guidelines for Action, Diocese of Colombo.
Mission of the Church under eight headings. (English, Sinhala, Tamil)
Available from: National Christian Council, Bishop's Office, 368/3A Bauddhaloka, Mawatha, Colombo 7, Sri Lanka.
Province/diocese: Church of Ceylon, Colombo.

Improving the Structures and Strategies for Evangelism.
Booklet on strategies for evangelism in the Diocese of Ijebu.
Available from: Diocese of Ijebu, Bishopscourt, PO Box 112, Ijebu-Ode, Nigeria.
Province/diocese: Nigeria, Ijebu.

Learning through Doing, Job Currie.
Methods of analysis/research.
Available from: R C Library IDEAS, Madurai, India.
Province/diocese: CSI India, Madurai and Ramnad.

Making Christ Known, The Revd Canon Philip King.
Plans and projects of some dioceses, deaneries and parishes during the Decade of Evangelism. It includes discussion questions and resource agencies.
Available from: The Board of Mission, Church House, Great Smith Street, London SW1P 3NZ, UK.
Province/diocese: Church of England Board of Mission.

Making the Most of the Millennium, various authors.
Good ideas and resources for outreach during the millennium.
Available from: CPAS, Athena Drive, Tachbrook Park, Warwick, CV34 6NG, UK.
Province/diocese: England, Coventry.

Turning Vision into Action, Kew and White, Cowley Pub.
Return to biblical mission imperative to turn the Church into vital body.
Available from: Diocesan Resource Library, Diocese of Texas, 3203 West Alabama, Houston, Texas 77098, USA
Province/diocese: ECUSA, Texas.

Vision Bearers, Richard Kew and Cyril Okorocha.
Drawing from examples around the world the authors show that evangelism is everywhere and in every context.
Available from: Anglican Communion Office, Partnership House, 157 Waterloo Road, London SE1 8UT.
Province/diocese: Anglican Communion Office.

Where do we go from here?, Philip Morris
A planning process in mission for Parochial Church Councils.
Available from: Church in Wales Publications, Church in Wales Centre, Woodland Place, Penarth, CF6 2EX, Wales.
Province/diocese: Church in Wales.

Training in evangelism

Before We Go.
A six-session study course on evangelism, faith, holiness and community life, for small groups; audio tapes/leader's guide.

Available from: Diocesan Church House, 211 New Church Road, Hove, BN3 4ED, UK.
Province/diocese: England, Chichester.

Courses in Evangelism, Christian Life and Service.
Training course with self-study material (available in many languages).
Available from: SEAN International, Park House, 191 Stafford Road, Wallington, Surrey, SM6 9BT, UK.
Province/diocese: Southern Africa, St Mark the Evangelist.

Creating Confidence in Evangelism, John Young.
Preparing for Evangelism; the hows and whys of evangelism; helping.
Available from: CPAS, Athena Drive, Tachbrook Park, Warwick, CV34 6NG, UK.
Province/diocese: England, Southwark.

Evangelism Explosion.
Evangelism training course.
Available from: EE Oceania Ministries, PO Box 168, Port Kembla 2505, Australia.
Province/diocese: Anglican Church of Australia.

Equipping the Saints – Evangelism, Diocesan Lay Training Committee, Kuala Lumpur.
Diocese of West Malaysia module on evangelism diocesan lay training.
Available from: Bishop Moses Ponniah, No 5 Jalan Mustaffa, Johor Bahru, Johor 80100, Malaysia. e-mail prteo@pl.jaring.my
Province/diocese: South East Asia, West Malaysia.

Evangelism Lessons, Canon Matthew Kale.
Topical study lessons on evangelism.
Available from: Diocese of Ysabel, PO Box 6, Buala, Solomon Islands.
Province/diocese: Melanesia, Ysabel.

Evangelism Made Slightly Less Difficult, Derek Tidball.
Practical guide for Christians wanting to use the Bible in mission and evangelism.

Available from: The Bible Society, Stonehill Green, Westlea, Swindon, SN5 7DG, UK.
Province/diocese: Church of England Board of Mission.

Evangelism Today, Revd K. M. J. Fernando.
Six Bible studies (English, Sinhala, Tamil).
Available from: National Christian Council, Bishop's Office, 368/3A Bauddhaloka, Mawath, Colombo 7, Sri Lanka.
Province/diocese: Church of Ceylon, Colombo.

Everyday Evangelism, Stephen Abbott.
Evangelism training, student and leader's manuals.
Available from: Dept of Evangelism, PO Box A295, Sydney South 1235, Australia.
Province/diocese: Anglican Church of Australia.

Extension Education.
Forty unit courses on many aspects of mission, evangelism, discipleship and training.
Available from: The Association for TEE, PO Box 520, Fraser Town, Bangalore, 560005, India.
Province/diocese: Church of South India.

Go Listen and Tell, Commission on Evangelism.
Evangelism training course for six sessions.
Available from: Diocese of Connecticut, 1335 Asylum Ave, Hartford, CT 06105-2295, USA.
Province/diocese: USA, Connecticut.

Join in the Jubilee, Philip Morris.
Three-session course to prepare for the millennium.
Available from: Church in Wales Publications, Church in Wales Centre, Woodland Place, Penarth, CF6 2EX, Wales.
Province/diocese: Church in Wales.

Lay Training Programmes, Diocese of Sabah and Singapore.
Twenty-unit lay evangelism training course aimed at developing practical skills for ministry and spiritual growth.
Available from: Diocese of Singapore, 4 Bishopsgate, Singapore, 247790.
Province/diocese: South East Asia, Sabah and Singapore.

Leading Children.
Understanding children of today, and bringing the Christian faith to a new generation. A short course for individuals or groups.
Available from: St John's College Extension Studies, Chilwell Lane, Bramcote, Beeston, Nottingham, NG9 3RL, UK. www.stjohnsnottm.ac.uk
Province/diocese: Church of England.

Liberal Evangelism, The Rt Revd John Saxbee.
Positive plea for generosity and respect in evangelism.
Available from: SPCK, Holy Trinity Church, Marylebone Road, London NW1 4DU, UK.
Province/diocese: England, Rochester.

Lost for Words, James Lawrence.
Six-week course on faith-sharing. How to speak about your faith in a natural and helpful way.
Available from: CPAS, Athena Drive, Tachbrook Park, Warwick, CV34 6NG, UK.
Province/diocese: England, Coventry.

Manual para Evangelismo en la Iglesia Local, The Revd John A. Macdonald and the Revd Rancisco Guardada.
Practical guide for evangelism in the local church (in Spanish).
Available from: Diocese of Honduras, Apartado 586, San Pedro Sula, Honduras, Central America.
Province/diocese: ECUSA, Honduras.

Modules on Evangelism, Diocese of West Malaysia.
Lay training course in evangelism.
Available from: Diocese of West Malaysia, 14 Pesiatan Stonor, 50450 Kuala Lumpur, West Malaysia.
Province/diocese: South East Asia, West Malaysia.

One Generation from Extinction?, The Primate's Commission on Evangelism.
Conversations on Congregational Vitality with George Carey; video with a study guide for three sessions.
Available from: Anglican Book Centre, 600 Jarvis Street, Toronto M4Y 2J6, Canada.
Province/diocese: Anglican Church of Canada.

Servant Evangelism.
A video on evangelism training.
Available from: Diocese of Southern Virginia Evangelism Officer,
600, Talbot Hall Road, Norfolk, VA 23505, USA.
Province/diocese: ECUSA, Southern Virginia.

Sunday/Monday.
Faith at work course. Used very widely with various groups.
Includes guidance for praise, prayer and suggestions for action.
Available from: Scripture Union, 207 Queensway, Bletchley,
Milton Keynes MK2 2EB, UK.
Province/diocese: England, Chelmsford.

The Mission of Evangelism, The Rt Revd Benjamin Kwashi.
Book on evangelism with Bible study guide and worksheets.
Available from: Pastoral Publications Commission, Diocese of Jos,
Bishopscourt, PO Box 6283, Jos, Plateau State, Nigeria.
Province/diocese: Nigeria, Jos.

Time Travelling, Paul Morris.
Video, audio cassettes, handbook all about time travelling. This
initiative has brought together a team of people in this diocese
ready to reach out to the youth.
Available from: Diocese of Southwell, Paul Morris, 39 Davies
Road, Nottingham NG2 5JE, UK.
Province/diocese: England, Southwell.

Training Manuals in Evangelism, various authors.
Basic material in evangelism and discipleship.
Available from: Life Ministries, Church of Uganda, Kampala,
Uganda.
Province/diocese: Uganda, Kigezi.

Training People Ready for Evangelism and Discipleship Training, Fr
Albert Chama.
A paper.
Available from: Diocese of Northern Zambia, PO Box 20173,
Kitwe, Zambia.
Province/diocese: Province of Central Africa.

Sharing your faith

Becoming a Contagious Christian, Mitelberg, Stridel and Hybels.
Training in sharing our faith with others.
Available from: Zondervan Press, STL Ltd, PO Box 300, Kingstown, Broadway, Carlisle CA3 0QS, UK.
Province/diocese: ECUSA, Fond du Lac.

Good News is for Sharing, David C. Cook.
Exploring ways to share faith effectively.
Available from: Diocesan Resource Library, Diocese of Texas, 3203 West Alabama, Houston, Texas 77098, USA.
Province/diocese: ECUSA, Texas.

Good News People, Harold Percy.
An introduction to evangelism for tongue-tied Christians. Helping people reflect their own experience.
Available from: Anglican Book Centre, 600 Jarvis Street, Toronto, ON M4Y 2J8, Canada.
Province/diocese: Anglican Church of Canada.

How to Give Away your Faith, Paul Little.
The nature and content of the Christian message and how to reach people where they are.
Available from: InterVarsity Press, Norton Street, Nottingham, NG7 3HR, UK.
Province/diocese: ECUSA, Connecticut.

How to Share your Faith without being Offensive, Joyce Neville.
How to share your faith in a gentle way to individuals and small groups.
Available from: Morehouse Publishing, USA (local bookshop).
Province/diocese: ECUSA, Connecticut.

'On the Move with Christ' (video), Anglican Communion Office.
Video portraying evangelism around the Communion with study guide.
Available from: Committee on World Mission, Diocese of Virginia, 110 W Franklin Street, Richmond, Virginia 23220, USA.
Province/diocese: ECUSA, Virginia.

Out of the Salt Shaker, Rebecca Manley Pippert.
Conversational style evangelism.

Available from: InterVarsity Press, Norton Street, Nottingham, NG7 3HR, UK.
Province/diocese: ECUSA, Connecticut.

'Person to Person' (video), The Bible Society.
Sharing your faith in Christ.
Available from: Scripture Union, 207 Queensway, Bletchley, Milton Keynes, MK2 2EB, UK.
Province/diocese: Many dioceses worldwide.

Personal Evangelism.
Study course in sharing our faith with individuals.
Available from: Christian Heritage Publishing, USA.
Province/diocese: Nigeria, Calabar.

Saints in Evangelism, Anglican Renewal Ministries.
Easy to apply teaching on friendship evangelism.
Available from: ARM Canada, 403 13th Street, Brandon, Manitoba, Canada R0M 0N0.
Province/diocese: Anglican Church of Canada.

Two Ways to Live, Philip Jensen.
Personal evangelism training with manuals.
Available from: Matthias Press, PO Box 225, Kingsford 2032, Australia.
Province/diocese: Anglican Church of Australia.

Won by One, Geoffrey Wallis.
Personal evangelism.
Available from: Diocese of Guildford, Willow Grange, Woking Road, Guildford, Surrey, GU4 7QS, UK.
Province/diocese: England, Guildford.

Cross-cultural

Entering Another's World.
How to live for God in another culture. A short course for individuals/groups.
Available from: St John's College Extension Studies, Chilwell Lane, Bramcote, Beeston, Nottingham NG9 3RL, UK.
www.stjohnsnottm.ac.uk
Province/diocese: St John's College, England.

Something in Common, Adrian Chatfield.
An introduction to the principles and practices of worldwide Anglicanism. A short course for individuals/groups.
Available from: St John's College Extension Studies, Chilwell Lane, Bramcote, Beeston, Nottingham NG9 3RL, UK. www.stjohnsnottm.ac.uk
Province/diocese: St John's College, England.

The World Christian.
How to live as members of the worldwide Church. A short course for individuals or groups.
Available from: St John's College Extension Studies, Chilwell Lane, Bramcote, Beeston, Nottingham NG9 3RL, UK. www.stjohnsnottm.ac.uk
Province/diocese: St John's College, England.

Laity

Basics: Student and Leader's Manuals, Evangelism Department.
Book 1, series of three – study course presenting the basics of the Christian faith and Anglican practice.
Available from: Church of Melanesia, PO Box 19, Honiara, Solomon Islands.
Province/diocese: The Church of the Province of Melanesia.

Introducing the Bible, Diocese of Sabah and Singapore.
Twenty-unit lay evangelism training course aimed at developing practical skills for ministry and spiritual growth.
Available from: Diocese of Singapore, 4 Bishopsgate, Singapore 247790.
Province/diocese: South East Asia, Sabah and Singapore.

Lay Training Course, Diocese of West Malaysia.
Lay training course in evangelism.
Available from: Diocese of West Malaysia, 14 Pesiatan Stonor, 50450 Kuala Lumpur, West Malaysia.
Province/diocese: South East Asia, West Malaysia.

Lay Training Programmes, Diocese of Sabah and Singapore.
Thirteen-unit lay biblical studies course covering the whole Bible, aimed at developing a practical understanding of the teaching of the Bible.

Available from: Diocese of Singapore, 4 Bishopsgate, Singapore 247790.
Province/diocese: South East Asia, Sabah and Singapore.

Leadership

A Handbook for Synod Delegates, Ijebu Diocesan Training Programme Committee.
Triennial seminar course for synod delegates.
Available from: Diocese of Ijebu, Bishopscourt, PO Box 112, Ijebu-Ode, Nigeria.
Province/diocese: Nigeria, Ijebu.

A Manual for Parish Councillors, Ijebu Diocesan Programme Committee.
Annual seminar course for parish councillors.
Available from: Diocese of Ijebu, Bishopscourt, PO Box 112, Ijebu-Ode, Nigeria.
Province/diocese: Nigeria, Ijebu.

Advanced: Student and Leader's Manuals, Provincial Evangelism Department.
Book 3 in series of three. Study course on leadership in the church, clergy and laity.
Available from: Church of Melanesia, PO Box 19, Honiara, Solomon Islands.
Province/diocese: The Church of the Province of Melanesia.

Evangelism Briefing Sheets, Diocese of Southwark.
A series of brief articles from different sources and cultures providing sitmulating background material for church leaders and those engaged in evangelism.
Available from: Diocese of Southwark, The Revd Jerry Lepine, St Matthews House, 100 George Street, Croydon CR0 1PE, UK.
Province/diocese: England, Southwark.

From Survival to Celebration, Howard Hanchey.
Leadership for the confident church.
Available from: Diocese of Southern Virginia, Evangelism Officer, 600 Talbot Hall Road, Norfolk, VA 23505, USA.
Province/diocese: ECUSA, Southern Virginia.

Tools for Evangelism

Books

Brushing up on Believing, Shelagh Brown and Gavin Reid.
A fresh look at basic Christianity and prayer.
Available from: Bible Reading Fellowship, Peter's Way, Sandy
Lane West, Oxford, OX4 5HG, UK.
Province/diocese: Anglican Communion Office.

El Hombre Life, Alfred Cooper.
The gospel for today.
Available from: The Revd Alfred Cooper, Casilla 50675, CC,
Santiago, Chile.
Province/diocese: Southern Cone, Chile.

The Case against Christ, John Young.
Resourceful book looking at some of the most common arguments
as to why people are/are not Christians.
Available from: Hodder & Stoughton, 338 Euston Road, London
NW1 3BH, UK.
Province/diocese: England, York.

Sadhu Sundar Singh, T. Dayanansan Francis (ed.).
Life and teaching of an Indian saint.
Available from: STL Ltd, PO Box 300, Kingstown, Broadway,
Carlisle CA3 0QS, UK.
Province/diocese: CNI India, Barrackpore.

Introduction to Christianity: videos

'Evangelismo Concepto y objective', John Macdonald.
Video to use in evangelism in the local church (in Spanish).
Available from: Diocese of Honduras, Apartado 586, San Pedro
Sula, Honduras, Central America.
Province/diocese: ECUSA, Honduras.

'Jesus Video'.
Video on the life of Jesus for non-Christians.
Available from: Agapé Resources, CPAS, Athena Drive, Tach-
brook Park, Warwick, CV34 6NG, UK.
Province/diocese: England, CPAS.

'Jesus Video Project'.
Video starter pack to use with taking the Jesus video into your community.
Available from: Agapé Resources, CPAS, Athena Drive, Tachbrook Park, Warwick, CV34 6NG, UK.
Province/diocese: England, CPAS.

'The House on the Rock', Stephen Cottrell and Diocese of Wakefield.
A video for ministry and mission among children and young people.
Available from: Diocese of Wakefield, Church House, 1 South Parade, Wakefield, WF1 1LP, UK.
Province/diocese: England, Wakefield.

'What's a Christian?', Ian Knox.
Video on how to become a Christian.
Available from: The 40:3 Trust, PO Box 403, Coventry, CV3 6SW, UK.
Province/diocese: England, Coventry.

'You're Never Too Old', Mavis Wilson with Diocese of Guildford.
A video on spirituality and evangelism in later life.
Available from: Diocese of Guildford, Grayswood Studios, Clammer Hill, Grayswood, Surrey, GU27 2DZ, UK.
Province/diocese: England, Guildford.

Introduction to Christianity: courses

Alpha Course, Nicky Gumbel, Holy Trinity Brompton, UK.
Ten-week introduction to Christianity course for non-churchgoers.
Available from: Holy Trinity Brompton, Brompton Road, London, SW7 1JA, UK.
Province/diocese: Many dioceses worldwide.

Basics: Student and Leader's Manuals, Evangelism Department.
First in series of three. Study course presenting the basics of the Christian faith and Anglican practice.
Available from: Church of Melanesia, PO Box 19, Honiara, Solomon Islands.
Province/diocese: The Province of the Church of Melanesia.

Christianity Explained, Michael Bennett.
Practical introduction to the Christian faith.
Available from: Koorong Bookshop, c/o Diocese of Bunbury, PO Box 15, Bunbury 6231, Australia.
Province/diocese: Anglican Church of Australia.

Credo.
Introduction to Christianity from a Catholic tradition perspective. A seven-week course for non-churchgoers.
Available from: Church Union, 7 Tufton Street, London, SW1P 3QN, UK.
Province/diocese: England, Chelmsford.

Discovering, Following and Choosing Jesus Christ.
Various courses designed for non-Christians.
Available from: Rivertree Christian Ministries, PO Box 7665, Pittsburgh, PA 15214-0665, USA.
Province/diocese: ECUSA, Fond du Lac.

El Hombre Life, Alfred Cooper.
The gospel for today.
Available from: The Revd Alfred Cooper, Casilla 50675, CC, Santiago, Chile.
Province/diocese: Southern Cone, Chile.

Emmaus – The Way of Faith, The Bible Society.
An excellent discipleship training programme.
Available from: The Bible Society, Stonehill Green, Westlea, Swindon, SN5 7DG, UK.
Province/diocese: England, Chelmsford.

Faith Confirmed , Peter Jackson and Chris Wright.
An introduction to what Anglicans believe, presenting key elements of the Christian faith in an enjoyable way with good illustrations.
Available from: SPCK, Holy Trinity Church, Marylebone Road, London, NW1 4DU, UK.
Province/diocese: Anglican Communion Office.

Know your Faith, John Young.
Discussions based on the Creed for groups. Written especially for the Decade of Evangelism.

Available from: Hodder & Stoughton, 338 Euston Road, London, NW1 3BH, UK.
Province/diocese: England, York.

Teach Yourself Christianity, John Young.
Reader-friendly contemporary guide to orthodox Christian belief.
Available from: Monarch Publications, Broadway House, The Broadway, Crowborough, TN6 1HQ, UK.
Province/diocese: England, Rochester.

This is Our Faith, Jeffery John (ed.).
This takes a straightforward approach which is catholic in its doctrine, liberal in its inclusiveness and evangelical in its aim to explain and share our faith in the gospel.
Available from: Anglican Communion Office, Partnership House, 157 Waterloo Road, London, SE1 8UT, UK.
Province/diocese: Anglican Communion Office.

Social concerns

Sustaining the Earth.
Christian perspectives on the environment and things we can all do about it. A short course for individuals or groups.
Available from: St John's College Extension Studies, Chilwell Lane, Bramcote, Beeston, Nottingham, NG9 3RL, UK.
Province/diocese: St John's College, England.

Life Issues, Chris Wright.
An introduction to such issues as abortion, violence, sex, suffering, etc., that challenge young people and invites them to consider how Christians respond to the same challenges.
Available from: Lion Publishing, Sandy Lane West, Oxford, OX4 5HG, UK.

Church Growth

Body and Cell, Howard Astin.
A story of one Anglican church exploring cell church practice for contemporary mission.
Available from: CPAS, Athena Drive, Tachbrook Park, Warwick, CV34 6NG, UK.
Province/diocese: England, Coventry.

Building Missionary Congregations, Robert Warren.
A series of articles suggesting practical ways to move 'from maintenance to mission'.
Available from: Board of Mission, Church House, Great Smith St, London SE1P 3NZ, UK.
Province/diocese: England, Durham.

Churches in Rural Development, Peter Sartorius.
Guidelines for action in community development.
Available from: Library, Tamilnadu Theological Seminary, Madurai, India.
Province/diocese: CSI India, Madurai and Ramnad.

Gukura kw' Itorrero rya Uganda muri Muhabura Diocese, The Rt Revd E. K. Shalita.
The growth of the Church in Bufumbira.
Available from: Diocesan Bookshop, c/o Church of Uganda, PO Box 22, Kisoro, Uganda.
Province/diocese: Uganda, Muhabura.

Lay Participation in the Growth of the Church, The Rt Revd A. O. Awosan.
Presidential address.
Available from: Diocese of Oke-Osun, PO Box 251, Gbongan, Nigeria.
Province/diocese: Nigeria, Oke-Osun.

More than Numbers, Loren Mead.
Church growth.
Available from: Diocese of Southern Virginia, Evangelism Officer, 600 Talbot Hall Road, Norfolk, VA 23505, USA.
Province/diocese: ECUSA, Southern Virginia.

Small Christian Communities, Thomas A. Kleissler, Margo A. LeBert and Mary C. McGuinness.
The building of small Christian communities.
Available from: Paulist Press, 997 Macarthur Boulevard, Mahway, New Jersey 07430, USA.
Province/diocese: West Africa, Kumasi.

Wholeness in Christ, Ministry of Evangelism and Spiritual Growth.
Weekend parish event – focus on parish renewal.

Available from: Diocese of Brandon, 341 13th Street, Brandon, Manitoba R7A 4P8, Canada.
Province/diocese: Anglican Church of Canada.

Willow Creek Seeker Service, G. A. Pritchard.
Methods of church growth in Willow Creek (church).
Available from: Willow Creek Community Church, 67 East Alogonauin Road, South Barrington, IL 60010, USA. website: www.willowcreek.org
Province/diocese: ECUSA, Florida.

Dry Bones Can Live Again, Robert E. Coleman.
A study manual on revival in the local church.
Available from: Old Tappan, New Jersey, USA.
Province/diocese: West Africa, Kumasi.

Making Your Church More Inviting, Oswald Alban Institute.
How congregations can invite and incorporate new members in the church.
Available from: Diocese of Aberdeen and Orkney, Diocesan Centre, 39 Kings Crescent, Aberdeen AB24 3HP, Scotland, UK.
Province/diocese: Scotland, Aberdeen and Orkney.

Appendix A
Memorandum Re Anglican Congress

DATE: April 22, 1999
TO: The Secretary General of the Anglican Communion
FROM: MISSIO: The Mission Commission of the Anglican
        Communion
RE: A FOURTH ANGLICAN CONGRESS

Dear Canon Peterson,

We are most grateful for your presence with us here in Harare, at this the final meeting of our mandate. Among the many subjects we have prayed over and discussed, we have taken particular interest in the proposal for another Anglican Congress, which we understand may take place in the year 2003. If carried forward, this would be only the fourth such congress in the history of the Anglican Communion – indeed, the Third Anglican Congress was held more than a generation ago. That congress, meeting in Toronto, will forever be known for having given birth to the rich concept of MRI – Mutual Responsibility and Interdependence in the Body of Christ. We believe that a fourth congress offers the promise of an equally fruitful summation of the mission of God in our time, into the service of which we are each commissioned by baptism.

In the interest, then, of seeing the proposal for a fourth Anglican congress move forward, we of MISSIO wish to offer the following thoughts and suggestions:

1 Theme: Meeting in Ely in 1996, MISSIO reaffirmed Resolution 44 of ACC-9 on the Decade of Evangelism, in particular section (g), which called for 'a significant Communion-wide celebration of the renewal of our commitment to mission and evangelism'. MISSIO urged that this theme be integral to the proposed congress. The 1998 Lambeth Conference, in turn, urged that the momentum of the Decade of Evangelism not be lost.

2 Planning Team: At our Recife meeting, in 1997, MISSIO stated

again our Ely resolution, noting the profound missiological significance of the Toronto Congress in its formulation of MRI. We expressed the hope that when a future planning committee is named, those named reflect the diversity of the Communion as well as its missionary experience. MISSIO offered to make available some of its own members for the task of planning.

3 Mission and Purpose Statement: You shared with us here in Harare notes towards a statement of mission and purpose for a fourth Anglican congress, prepared last year by ACC member Judith Conley and yourself. MISSIO wishes particularly to underline your conviction that a clear, strong and easily understandable mission/purpose statement should be written, a plan with achievable goals and objectives. Recalling earlier congresses in Minneapolis and Toronto, you and Mrs Conley stated: 'The vision which comes out of the Congress must be owned and understood by everyone. The Anglican Congress should engage and include "all sorts of conditions" of people. The real test will be to ask how does this Congress benefit the Communion as a global church.'

4 Cost: MISSIO understands that a Communion-wide congress coming midway between Lambeth Conferences will require significant efforts to organize and fund. With regard to the latter requirement, we believe the congress can be largely self-funded; that, given sufficient time and encouragement, most if not all diocesan delegations will raise the funds necessary for their participation. For this reason, we hope planners will keep their focus on the promise and opportunity the congress will present and not be unduly deterred by financial considerations.

5 Factors to Balance: Along with the Archbishop of Canterbury, MISSIO wishes to see strong lay participation in the congress. Gender and age balance must not be neglected – the congress will be a formative experience for youth. Provision should be made for the participation of voluntary movements, religious orders and specialist ministries.

6 Other Models: MISSIO urges the planners to review other large Christian gatherings for innovative and practical models. We think of the German Kirchentag and the gatherings of the Commission on World Mission and Evangelism (of the World Council of Churches) in San Antonio, Texas and Salvador,

Brazil, especially the provisions for accredited observers/visitors and a preparatory process for the participants.

7 Prior Conference: Finally, we shared with you our expectations that a conference of mission agencies (synodical, provincial and voluntary) will convene by the end of 2001. Fifteen years after a similar gathering in Brisbane, the conference will reflect on the roles and responsibilities of the mission agencies, as well as promote networking and mutual understanding among the older agencies and newer expressions of mission structures. MISSIO hopes congress planners will see the outcome of the mission agencies conference as informing and enriching the Fourth Anglican Congress, as we believe it will.

As MISSIO completes its five-year mandate, we will pass on to our successor commission our desire that it commit itself to making the next Anglican congress a reality and a success.

Appendix B
Ten Priorities in Evangelism

(From the MISSIO Report on the Mid-Point Review of
the Decade of Evangelism)

The reports from around the Communion identified the following
issues as priorities to be addressed in the second half of the Decade.

Priorities

1 Issues of Training and Nuture
The issue identified as top priority was the need to revise the training, nurture and formation of clergy, so as to prepare them to
participate and give leadership in evangelism. Equipping and
empowering the laity was also emphasized. Both clergy and laity
need opportunities to gain confidence in telling their faith stories.
Clergy in particular need encouragement and help to engage in
on-going theological formation.

2 Issues of Spirituality and Worship
There was a strong call for freer worship and contextualized
liturgy. Our common pattern of Anglican liturgy has helped to
bind us together, but needs to be revised to reflect local cultures.
Evangelistic endeavours need to be undertaken under the
guidance of the Holy Spirit, and should be strongly supported
and surrounded by personal and corporate prayer. Personal
devotion and communal worship lie at the heart of renewal in
evangelism – which often includes 'spiritual warfare'. Clergy and
lay leaders need training in this direction.

3 Repentance and Humility
There was an acknowledgement that humble repentance is a
necessary precondition to bold evangelism. In each part of the
Communion there is a need for the Church to repent of its past
and present sins, and this is an on-going process which may in
some cases involve restitution.

4 The Role of Lay People

The central role of the laity in evangelism was strongly affirmed. There is a need not merely to give tasks to lay people, but rather, to empower them by truly delegating authority and encouraging and enabling them to get on with the job in their homes, places of work and daily lives. The important role of women in witness was particularly highlighted. In many parts of Africa, especially West Africa, women lead the Church's mission in its social and spiritual aspects, largely through the work of Mothers' Union.

5 A Church Open To All People

Local congregations/Christian communities need to become more welcoming, nurturing and open to all people. They also need to provide neighbourhood, house-oriented or 'cell' groups which newcomers can join. The hierarchical structures of our Anglican Church need to be modified to allow a more equitable sharing of responsibilities.

6 Leadership and Visioning

Delegates called for strong and prophetic leadership from the bishops of the Communion. There is a need for bishops to demonstrate their commitment to evangelism, and to articulate a clear evangelistic vision. They carry a responsibility as vision bearers for the Communion.

7 Youth

There was a strong call to explore and harness ways of ministering with the youth, both implementing whatever changes are needed in order to attract youth, as well as the need for affirming and encouraging youth in the work of evangelism and in their spiritual and moral formation.

8 Co-operation with other Christians

Mention was made of evangelism in co-operation with other churches or individual non-Anglican Christians. In the second half of the Decade, provinces need to reassess their ecumenical co-operation in evangelism.

9 Other Faiths, Ideologies, Unreached People

There was special concern about strengthening our witness among people of other faiths. Mention was also made of the challenge of materialism and secularism. We should support efforts to reach the unreached both in the modern and mega cities of the wealthier parts of the world and in the less developed places.

10   Issues of Social and Environmental Justice

Evangelism is the central task given to the Church, and it was felt that this means a call to live like Christ in concern for the poor, the weak, the oppressed and the creation, and in working to overcome structures and systems that perpetuate poverty, oppression and environmental degradation. Within the Church it was felt that provinces and dioceses should reflect their commitment to the vision of becoming a movement for mission by giving mission a priority place in their budgeting.

Practical Suggestions for Mobilizing the Church

Working groups at the conference suggested some practical ways to help the Church address the emerging issues and future directions identified above. These suggestions need to be adapted to fit local situations.

1   Seminary Training

There needs to be a Communion-wide review and revision of seminary curricula and staffing to prioritize evangelism. To shift the Church from maintenance to mission, we need to put mission at the heart and as the motivating force in ministerial formation.

2   Exchanges of Personnel

These exchanges should increase, and can happen in a variety of ways and in all directions.

3   Team and Group Visits

These are short-term, focused visits, to meet specific requests.

4   Translation and Adaptation of Resources

There is a need for more resources in languages other than English, and in culturally sensitive adaptations.

5   Sharing Stories

We would be helped by hearing one another's stories, including faith stories and accounts of successful and unsuccessful efforts in evangelism.

6   Regional Gatherings

Gatherings are one of the important ways we meet each other, encourage and support each other, exchange our stories, and celebrate our oneness and rich diversity.

7 Electronic Networking
We need to make the best possible use of the technology that is available.

8 Evangelism Assessment/Evaluation
This process involves setting measurable goals and then assessing how well we are doing in fulfilling these.

9 Budgets
The Church at all levels should budget sufficient funds to enable the work of evangelism. Examining our budgets is one way of measuring our commitment to evangelism.

10 Mission Structures and Programmes
The programmes and structures, which have been established to assist the Church throughout the Communion to fulfil its broad mission goals, should be modified as necessary to assist with current evangelism needs.

11 Ecumenical Endeavours
Local parishes and dioceses need to be encouraged to approach the evangelistic task ecumenically, in co-operation with other Christians in their own communities.

Questions to Help Us Move Forward

These questions are intended to stimulate thought, leading to positive action. They should be adapted as necessary for local situations.

For the Anglican Consultative Council

1 Sharing of Resources
What and where are the identifiable resources, human and material, that can be used for evangelism, and how can these be effectively shared around the Communion?

2 Language and Translation
Are some language groups in the Communion being marginalized in the study of theology and at conferences, and what can be done to correct this anomaly?

3   Funding
Does the evangelism budget adequately reflect the priority of this
Decade of Evangelism?

For Bishops/Dioceses

1   Vision and Encouragement
Evangelism is the cutting edge of mission. What is your vision for
the spread of the gospel, recruitment, training and sending of
labourers for the on-going task of mission? (See MISSIO's letter
to the Bishops of the Commission.)

2   Training
How central is the practical training in evangelism in the
curriculum of your institutions of lay and clergy training?

3   Relevant Liturgy
How do you encourage your people to adapt liturgy to better
reflect your culture and the local situation and to make worship a
more lively and creative encounter with God?

For Parishes

1   Sensitivity to Local Needs
What do people find attractive in your congregation?

2   Welcoming Community
In what ways can you improve your welcome to others?

3   Building Confidence for Evangelism
How does your parish help members to share their faith at home,
at work, with neighbours and in the wider society?

For all

Look at the list of emerging issues and practical suggestions. In
each list which are the top three priorities for you in your
situation? Do you have any other priorities? What will you do
about them?

Appendix C
Ten Principles of Partnership

1   Local Initiative

'The responsibility for mission in any place belongs primarily to the church in that place' (ACC-2, p. 53). Thus the initiative for establishing a new missionary venture in any given place belongs to the local church. Partnership therefore implies respect for the authority of the local church.

2   Mutuality

Mutuality is underscored by a deep sense of open and joint accountability. 'To be open to one another as friends on the basis of common commitment, mutual trust, confession and forgiveness, keeping one another informed of all plans and programmes and submitting ourselves to mutual accountability and correction' (*Sharing Life – El Escorial – Guidelines for Sharing*, 1987, World Council of Churches, p. 29).

Mutuality in partnership affirms the oneness of the people of God, their unity and inter-relatedness as the children of one Father. In this relationship each person and community is recognized, valued, affirmed and respected.

In decision-making, mutuality means sharing power. For example, major decisions affecting partners (in the South) should not be taken without their participation in the decision whether by their presence when it is made or by prior consultation.

3   Responsible Stewardship

Responsible stewardship in partnership means that partners see their resources as jointly owned and held in trust by each member for the common good (1 Cor. 12.7). The giving, receiving and use of resources must be controlled by judiciousness, selflessness, maturity and responsibility (2 Cor. 8.9).

God's gifts to any one part of the universal Church are given in trust for the mission of the whole church. No mission agency, diocese, province or national church 'owns' its resources.

4 Interdependence

'Interdependence means to represent to one another our needs and problems in relationships where there are no absolute donors, or absolute recipients, but all have needs to be met and gifts to give' (WCC, *Sharing Life*, p. 29).

We need each other. We are incomplete and cannot be called the Church of God if the diversity implicit in our catholicity is overtaken by a parochial, cultural or racial homogeneity. In practice, three consequences follow:

i   every cultural group has something to give or something others can learn from them;
ii all cultures need redeeming and therefore no culture can be said to be fundamentally Christian and thus superior to others;
iii everyone has needs that can only be met by others. There is an African saying addressed to arrogant and selfish rich people: 'No one buries himself — if he does one of his hands will be outside the grave.'

5 Cross Fertilization

Cross fertilization requires a willingness to learn from one another. It produces an enrichment that results from being open to one another's ideas, experiences and respecting one another's cultural and contextual pecularities in a process of give and take. 'If we once acted as though there were only givers who had nothing to receive and receivers who had nothing to give, the oneness of the missionary task must now make us both givers and receivers' (ACC-2, p. 53).

6 Integrity

A healthy partnership calls for integrity at all levels. It involves a recognition that all partners are essentially equal. This implies a commitment to be real and honest. We do not always have to say 'yes' to everything the other partner says for fear of offending or out of a false sense of guilt. A healthy partnership requires that we take each other seriously, raise creative and loving challenges that could lead to positive re-evaluation of long held traditions and assumptions. The result is a healthier and more enriching relationship. This includes both listening to each other and being willing to repent and change where we have been in error.

7   Transparency

Transparency involves openness and honesty with one another. It also involves risks. The risk of being hurt. The risk of being misunderstood and the risk of being taken advantage of.

Information needs to be fully shared with one another; not only information connected with our specific relationship with one another but information about all of our relationships. Full disclosure of financial information to one another is one of the marks of a transparent relationship.

8   Solidarity

We are part of each other. We are committed to one another in Christ's body. What touches one member touches the others. Thus no one member must be left to suffer alone. In many non-western cultures, group cohesion and solidarity are thought to be central to existence and crucial to the progress and survival of society. In spite of their strong belief in the rights and individuality of the individual, the Igbo of Nigeria, for example, argue that 'igwe bu ike' ('our strength has its source and sustenance in group solidarity'). In parts of East Africa, the Harambee motif has been successfully harnessed in political, social and religious spheres to achieve astounding results. Missiologically speaking the Church needs to act in solidarity 'so that the world may believe' (John 17.21).

9   Meeting Together

The concept of mutual responsibility and interdependence in the body of Christ implies that the Church in every place should find a forum for periodic evaluation, self-assessment and cross-cultural fertilization. Thus while a PIM consultation is not the fulfilment of a PIM vision, it is essential to it (ACC-2, p. 53). We need to meet together.

10   Acting Ecumenically

Our mission relationships as Anglicans must be seen as part of the wider mission relationships of all Christians. In this Decade MISAG-II underlines the importance of the Lambeth call for Anglicans to explore ways of being involved in mission co-operatively with other Christians. We need the stimulation, the critique and the encouragement of sisters and brothers in Christ of other traditions. A constant question before us must be, to what extent are those of other traditions invited to participate in advising and working with us in our outreach?

Mission Issues and Strategy Advisory Group II (MISAG II) *Towards Dynamic Mission: Renewing the Church for Mission*, 1993.

Appendix D
Apology and Covenant Documents

Nippon Sei Ko Kai

49th Regular General Synod, 23 May 1996
(Excerpt from Minutes)

Resolution No. 34
Statement on War Responsibility of Nippon Sei Ko Kai

1 The Nippon Sei Ko Kai, after 50 years since the end of World
War II, admits its responsibility and confesses its sin for having
supported and allowed, before and during the war, the colonial
rule and the war of aggression by the State of Japan.

In 1945, the Nippon Sei Ko Kai was at a historic turning
point – the end of Japan's invasion and colonial rule in the
Asia-Pacific region. At the special session of the 21st General
Synod held in the same year, Bishop Paul Shinji Sasaki
expressed the church's repentance for what it had done during
the war period, and pointed out that the church had chosen to
comply with the government policy and had forgotten its
mission. At that moment, the General Synod, as well as the
House of Bishops, the dioceses and parishes should also have
deeply repented for not having fulfilled their prophetic role.
They should also have made a sincere apology to their neighbours whom Japan had invaded and ruled, and should have
sought a truly reconciled relationship with them.

Since establishment, the Nippon Sei Ko Kai has been making
compromises with the idea of a Tenno (God in Heaven) ruled
nation and militarism which go against the gospel, and has not
been able to resist strongly against, or refuse those principles.
The Nippon Sei Ko Kai was oppressed by the authorities, and
some priests and lay people experienced the struggle of faith.
But despite these bitter experiences, our church has not been
able to stand beside those who are oppressed and suffering.
Despite its more recent internationalism, our church has not

been able to see Japan as an aggressor in the war. In fact, using the 'Special Prayer for the China Incident' and 'Special Prayer for the Greater East Asia War' (WWII), our church has justified Japan's rule over other ethnic groups and supported the war under the name of Christianity. We have been a closed church whose main concern is the expansion of the membership and the retention of the institution, this being unable to serve as the salt for the earth as indicated in the gospel.

2 The Nippon Sei Ko Kai confesses to God and apologizes to the people in Asia and the Pacific that we did not admit our fault immediately after the end of the war, were unaware of our responsibility for the past 50 years, and have not actively called for reconciliation and compensation until today.

At the 22nd General Synod in 1947, the Nippon Sei Ko Kai officially adopted *The Book of Common Prayer* issued in 1938. The book included prayers for the Tenno and 'Kigensetsu', which regarded the Tenno and his officials. During the Holy Communion, a priest prayed for God's blessing for all who had sovereignty, especially the Tenno. In this way, even after the war, the Nippon Sei Ko Kai continued to use *The Book of Common Prayer*, which justified the Tenno system of government as God's will. These are the major issues to be questioned with regard to the war responsibility, but the Church has neglected to change its attitude.

The Diocese of Okinawa has been telling the stories about massacres of Okinawan people and forced collective suicides among them, which occurred during the war as a result of the government policy to regard the people as subordinates of the Tenno. They have also been pointing out the threats of the US military bases in Okinawa throughout the post-war period. Before its transfer to the Nippon Sei Ko Kai in 1972, the Diocese of Okinawa had asked the Nippon Sei Ko Kai to understand Okinawa's history and its situation. The Nippon Sei Ko Kai must repent that it has neglected to respond to that call until today.

3 The Nippon Sei Ko Kai confesses that, even after the war, it has yet to get rid of discriminatory attitudes. We pray that we will be changed to recognize our mission to do justice as the people of God, and, as the vessels of peace, to listen to the voices of the divisions, pains, cries and sufferings of the world.

As a sign of repentance, we the people of the Nippon Sei Ko Kai will do the following:

1 to share the confession of our war responsibilities among all of the parishes
2 to convey an apology to the churches in the countries which Japan had invaded
3 to start and continue a programme in each diocese and parish, to review the historical facts and to deepen our understanding of the gospel.

(Extracted from the Minutes)

The Nippon Sei Ko Kai General Synod Secretary

Anglican Church of Canada

Anglican Leader Apologizes to Aboriginal People for Residential Schools

My Brothers and Sisters,
Together here with you I have listened as you have told your stories of the residential schools.
I have heard the voices that have spoken of pain and hurt experienced in the schools, and of the scars, which endure to this day.
I have felt shame and humiliation as I have heard of suffering inflicted by my people, and as I think of the part our church played in that suffering.
I am deeply conscious of the sacredness of the stories that you have told and I hold in the highest honour those who have told them.
I have heard with admiration the stories of people and communities who have worked at healing, and I am aware of how much healing is needed.
I also know that I am in need of healing, and my own people are in need of healing, and our church is in need of healing. Without that healing, we will continue the same attitudes that have done such damage in the past.
I also know that healing takes a long time, both for people and for communities.
I also know that it is God who heals, and that God can begin to heal when we open ourselves, our wounds, our failures and our

shame to God. I want to take one step along that path here and now.

I accept and I confess before God and you, our failures in the residential schools. We failed you. We failed ourselves. We failed God.

I am sorry, more than I can say, that we were part of a system, which took you and your children from home and family.

I am sorry, more than I can say, that we tried to remake you in our image, taking from you your language and the signs of your identity.

I am sorry, more than I can say, that in our schools so many were abused physically, sexually, culturally and emotionally.

On behalf of the Anglican Church of Canada, I present our apology.

I do this at the desire of those in the church like the National Executive Council, who know some of your stories and have asked me to apologize.

I do this in the name of many who do not know these stories.

And I do this even though there are those in the church who cannot accept the fact that these things were done in our name.

As soon as I am home, I shall tell all the bishops what I have said, and ask them to co-operate with me and with the National Executive Council in helping this healing at the local level.

Some bishops have already begun this work.

I know how often you have heard words which have been empty because they have not been accompanied by actions. I pledge to you my best efforts, and the efforts of our church at the national level, to walk with you along the path of God's healing.

The work of the Residential Schools Working Group, the video, the commitment and the effort of the special assistants to the primate for this work, the grants available for healing conferences, are some signs of that pledge, and we shall work for others.

This is Friday, the day of Jesus' suffering and death. It is the anniversary of the first atomic bomb at Hiroshima, one of the most terrible injuries ever inflicted by one people on another.

But even atomic bombs and Good Friday are not the last word. God raised Jesus from the dead as a sign that life and wholeness are the everlasting and unquenchable purpose of God.

Thank you for listening to me.

✝ Michael, Archbishop and Primate

Response to the Primate at the National Native Convocation
Delivered by Vi Smith on behalf of the elders and participants,
Minaki, Ontario, Saturday, August 7, 1993.

On behalf of this gathering, we acknowledge and accept
the apology that the Primate has offered on behalf of the
Anglican Church of Canada.
It was offered from his heart with sincerity, sensitivity, compassion and humility. We receive it in the same manner. We
offer praise and thanks to our Creator for his courage.
We know it wasn't easy. Let us keep him in our hearts and
prayers, that God will continue to give him the strength and
courage to continue with his tasks.

Text of the Covenant Statement

We, representatives of the indigenous people of the Anglican
Church of Canada, meeting in Winnipeg from the 23 to 26 of
April 1994, pledge ourselves to this covenant for the sake of
our people and in trust of our Lord and Saviour, Jesus
Christ:
Under the guidance of God's Spirit, we agree to do all we
can to call our people into unity in a new, self-determining
community within the Anglican Church of Canada.
To this end, we extend the hand of partnership to all those
who will help us build a truly Anglican Indigenous Church
in Canada.
May God bless this new vision and give us grace to accomplish it. Amen. [21 signatures]

Background to Covenant

Our Journey of Spiritual Renewal

We, the indigenous partners in Canada of the Anglican Communion respectfully affirm our place in God's Creation and in
God's Love, manifest through the Grace of Jesus Christ. In
specific, we address the Anglican Canadians with whom we
are in direct communion.
We have shared a journey of close to three centuries in which
we have been: denied our place in God's Creation, denied our

right as Children of God, treated as less than equal; and subjected to abuse, culturally, physically, emotionally, sexually and spiritually.

The result, in our communities, homes and daily lives, has been and continues to be: broken homes and lives; sexual and family violence; high recidivism and incarceration rates; high chemical abuse; loss of spiritual fulfilment; loss of cultures, languages and traditions; and poor stewardship of Mother Earth.

Because the national church's canons, structure and policies have not always responded to our needs nor heard our voice; we now claim our place and responsibility as equal partners in a new shared journey of healing moving towards wholeness and justice.

We acknowledge that God is calling us to a prayerful dialogue towards self-determination for us, the Indigenous people, within the Anglican Communion in Canada. Through this new relationship we can better respond to the challenges facing us in a relevant and meaningful way.

As faithful people of God, guided by the Holy Spirit, we invite you, the Anglican Communion of Canada, to convenant with us, the Indigenous Anglicans of Canada, in our vision of a new and enriched journey.

Resources

Bakare, S., *The Drumbeat of Life: Jubilee in an African Context*. WCC, Geneva, 1997.

Bosch, D. J., *Transforming Mission: Paradigm Shifts in Theology of Mission*. Orbis Books, Maryknoll, 1991.

Bowen, R., ... *So I Send You: A Study Guide to Mission*. SPCK, London, 1996.

Craston, C. (ed.), *By Word and Deed: Sharing the Good News through Mission*. Church House Publishing, London, 1992.

Dietterich, P. and Dietterich, I., *A Systems Model of the Church in Ministry and Mission*. Center for Parish Development, Chicago, 1994.

Duraisingh, C. (ed.), *Called to One Hope: The Gospel in Diverse Cultures*. WCC Publications, Geneva, 1998.

Guder, D. L. (ed.), *Missional Church: A Vision for the Sending of the Church in North America*. Eerdmans, Grand Rapids, 1998.

Lambeth Conference, *The Truth Shall Set You Free*. Report of the 1988 Lambeth Conference, Church House Publishing, London, 1988.

McCoy, M., 'Going in peace, or breaking in pieces? Anglican unity and the mission of God', *InterMission: An Australian Journal of Mission* 4/1 (February 1998), pp. 22–33.

MISAG I, *Giving Mission its Proper Place*. Report of the Mission Issues and Strategy Advisory Group I (MISAG I), Anglican Consultative Council, London, 1985.

MISAG II, *Towards Dynamic Mission: Renewing the Church for Mission*. Final report of the Second Mission Issues and Strategy Advisory Group (MISAG II), Anglican Consultative Council, London, 1993.

Nazir-Ali, M., *From Everywhere to Everywhere: A World View of Christian Mission*. Collins, London, 1990.

Okorocha, C. C. (ed.), *The Cutting Edge of Mission*. Report of the Mid-point Review of the Decade of Evangelism, Anglican Communion Office, London, 1996.

Shenk, W. R., *Write the Vision: The Church Renewed*. Trinity Press International, Valley Forge, Pa., 1995.

Taylor, J. V., *The Uncancelled Mandate: Four Bible Studies on Christian Mission for the Approaching Millennium*. Church House Publishing, London, 1998.

Van Engen, C., *Mission on the Way: Issues in Mission Theology*. Baker, Grand Rapids, 1996.

Warren, R., *Being Human, Being Church: Spirituality and Mission in the Local Church*. Marshall Pickering, London, 1995.

Notes

1 Janet Hodgson, 'Decade of transformation.' In Colin Craston (ed.), *By Word and Deed: Sharing the Good News through Mission*. Church House Publishing, London, 1992, pp. 14–32.

2 Paper by Dr Sebastião Gameleira Soares at MISSIO's third meeting (Recife, Brazil 1997).

3 In Latin America the word 'evangelization' is often used to describe the whole task of the Church's witness – what others might call 'mission'. It is broader than the more specific activity of evangelism.

4 South African theologian Albert Nolan, quoted by Janet Hodgson in Craston, *By Word and Deed*, p. 19.

5 Dr Vinay Samuel's comments as consultant to Section II of the 1998 Lambeth Conference, transcribed and distributed to the bishops.

6 *The Truth Shall Set You Free*. Report of the 1988 Lambeth Conference, Church House Publishing, London, p. 43.

7 Response to the Archbishop of Canterbury in *The Truth Shall Set You Free*, p. 292.

8 Report of Section IV, 1998 Lambeth Conference, p. 216.

9 John V. Taylor, *The Uncancelled Mandate: Four Bible Studies on Christian Mission for the Approaching Millennium*. Church House Publishing, London, 1998, p. 29.

10 The images are those of the Welsh poet R. S. Thomas.

11 Robert Warren, *Being Human, Being Church*. Marshall Pickering, London, 1995.

12 E.g. Robin Greenwood, *Transforming Priesthood: A New Theology of Mission and Ministry*. SPCK, London, 1994.

13 Darrell L. Guder (ed.) 1998. *Missional Church: A Vision for the Sending of the Church in North America*. Eerdmans, Grand Rapids, 1998, pp. 1–7.

14 Paul and Inagrace Dietterich, *A Systems Model of the Church in*

Ministry and Mission. Center for Parish Development, Chicago, 1994, pp. 6–11.

15 This discussion draws on Mike McCoy,'Going in peace, or breaking in pieces? Anglican unity and the mission of God', *InterMission: An Australian Journal of Mission* 4/1 (February 1998), pp. 22–33.

16 Kathy Galloway's comments to Section II of the 1998 Lambeth Conference, transcribed and distributed to the bishops.

17 Bishop Rowan Williams, Section chairman, in comments to Section II of the 1998 Lambeth Conference, transcribed and distributed to the bishops.

18 ARCIC, *Church as Communion.* Church House Publishing, London, 1991, para. 15.

19 From the Seventh WCC Assembly report, *The Unity of the Church as Koinonia: Gift and Calling.*

20 Frederick Denison Maurice, who distinguishes between gospel and religion, could help us a little more in this reflection. See the pre-Lambeth 1998 document, Section II, item 2.8, and the paper given by Sebastião Gameleira Soares to the Recife meeting of MISSIO, September 1997.

21 *Towards Dynamic Mission: Renewing the Church for Mission.* Report of MISAG II. Anglican Consultative Council, London, 1993, pp. 11–12.

22 Christopher Duraisingh (ed.), *Called to One Hope: The Gospel in Diverse Cultures.* WCC Publications, Geneva, 1998.

23 *Called to One Hope*, pp. 34–7.

24 Report of the 1998 Lambeth Conference, Section II.4, pp. 147–66.

25 Report of the 1998 Lambeth Conference, Section II.4, p. 157.

26 Report of the 1998 Lambeth Conference, Section II.4, p. 150.

27 These points are drawn from an unpublished paper by David Ford, 'What is the Diocese?' given at the Windsor Consultation, 5–7 February 1996, as reported by Tom Frame, 'The diocese and Anglican mission', *InterMission: An Australian Journal of Mission* 5/1 (February 1999), pp. 2–17.

28 *Report of the Primates' Meeting, Cyprus, 1989,* Appendix D 2a.

29 *The Cutting Edge of Mission: Report on the Mid-point Review of the Decade of Evangelism,* p. 130.

30 Address to Church of England Congress on Evangelism, March 1999.
31 *The Cutting Edge of Mission*, pp. 145–6.
32 *The Truth Shall Set You Free: Report of the 1988 Lambeth Conference*, Church House Publishing.
33 *The Cutting Edge of Mission: Report on the Mid-point Review of the Decade of Evangelism* dealt with full-time residential training, the study of the Bible and mission, mission and contextual theologies; mission, pastoral theology and other faiths, courses, theological education by extension and continuing training.
34 *Towards Dynamic Mission: MISAG II Report*, p. 36.
35 *Report of Anglican Congress, 1963*, p. 22.
36 *Report of ACC-2, Dublin, 1973*, p. 53.
37 *Towards Dynamic Mission: Renewing the Church for Mission*. Final report of MISAG II, 1993, p. 33.

Index

The Society for Promoting Christian Knowledge (SPCK) was
founded in 1698. Its mission statement is:

To promote Christian knowledge by

- **Communicating the Christian faith in its
  rich diversity**
- **Helping people to understand the Christian faith
  and to develop their personal faith; and**
- **Equipping Christians for mission and ministry**

SPCK Worldwide serves the Church through Christian
literature and communication projects in 100 countries, and
provides books for those training for ministry in many parts of
the developing world. This worldwide service depends upon the
generosity of others and all gifts are spent wholly on ministry
programmes, without deductions.

SPCK Bookshops support the life of the Christian community
by making available a full range of Christian literature and other
resources, providing support for those training for ministry, and
assisting bookstalls and book agents throughout the UK.

SPCK Publishing produces Christian books and resources,
covering a wide range of inspirational, pastoral, practical and
academic subjects. Authors are drawn from many different
Christian traditions, and publications aim to meet the needs of a
wide variety of readers in the UK and throughout the world.

The Society does not necessarily endorse the individual views
contained in its publications, but hopes they stimulate readers to
think about and further develop their Christian faith.

For information about the Society, visit our website at
www.spck.org.uk, or write to:
SPCK, Holy Trinity Church, Marylebone Road,
London NW1 4DU, United Kingdom.